CHUNG SANG-HWA

CHUNG SANG-HWA
EXCAVATIONS, 1964–78

CONTENTS

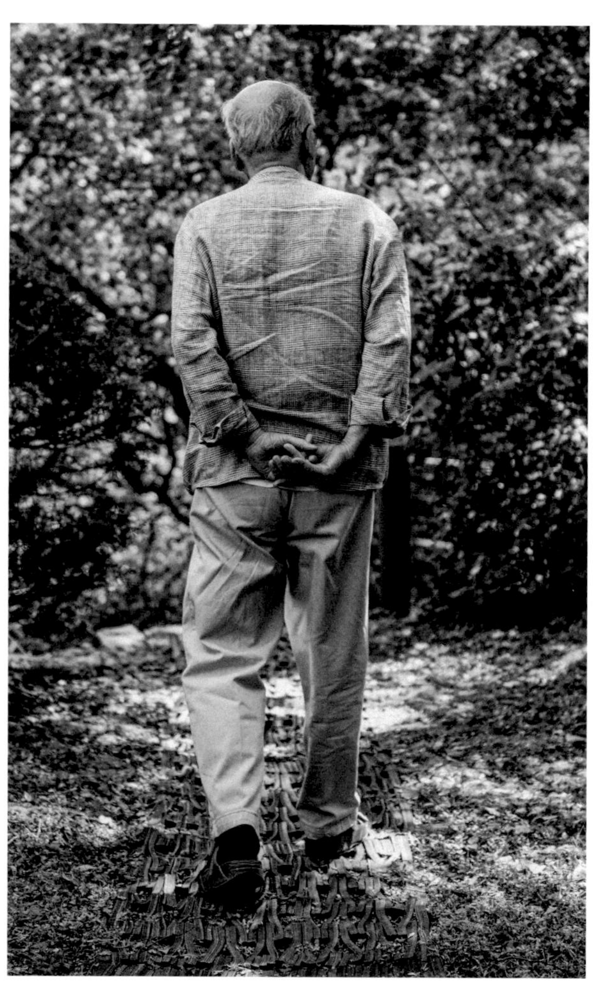

For Chung Sang-Hwa, process is paramount. Working alone in his studio, he begins by stretching fabric—a length of coarse canvas or jute—atop a wooden armature, stopping when he senses the rightness of its tension. Taking up paint—acrylics and oils thickened with kaolin and glue—he moves between addition and erasure, applying his medium to the raw support, then pulling portions away. Layers of paint or bare fabric emerge, engaging presence and absence in fugue-like rhythms. Subtle, handwrought details embed contingency into the surface, sensitizing the perception of maker and viewer alike. Marked by Chung's meditative attention, each painting relays deeper realms of significance and sensation, where aesthetics and philosophy meet.

The contours of this method—which Chung continues perfecting to this day—developed between the mid-1960s and early 1970s. This is the period that the present catalogue and exhibition explore. The title, *Excavations*, alludes to the artist's mode of making, which positions painting as a kind of archaeology—a composite of strata alternately laid bare and obscured. Yet it also expresses a broader ambition: a desire to "excavate" the monochromes of the mid-1970s onward, for which Chung is best known, tracing their conceits to a prior source—a time of searching and diffuse possibility. Together, these early paintings embody Chung's conviction that art's power inheres, not in external criteria such as imagery or language, but in its own insistent presence, forged through a labor of assiduous refinement.

Though anchored in the solitary space of his studio, Chung's art did not mature in isolation. In 1967, he left Korea seeking new spaces, both literal and figurative, for his practice. Living first in Paris and then Kobe, Japan, he joined the gestural thrust of Art Informel with the austerity of Minimalism, creating paintings that register the breakthroughs of the postwar years while settling into a style that would later be coined *Dansaekhwa*. Forged in the intersection among cultures and movements, his paintings find affinities with other artists in Lévy Gorvy's program: Günther Uecker, in his ruminative repetitions; Pat Steir, in her surrender of ego; and Pierre Soulages, in his courting of texture. Unburdened by preset theories, each poses abstraction as an open-ended question—a prompt to be continuously restated yet never resolved. While profoundly personal, Chung's art achieves the universal, nesting meaning within material, poetry within process.

We would like to thank all those who made this exhibition and publication possible.

First and foremost, our gratitude to the artist, Chung Sang-Hwa. The hours spent together discussing your paintings, your principles, and your life were a genuine gift. Your art offers not simply a singular approach to abstraction but a consummate way of being in the world, in which mind and body alike loosen into the focused flow of making.

Our sincere appreciation to the contributors to this catalogue: David McCann, for your sensitive translation of Shin Young-Bok's evocative verse, which graces a poster on the wall of Chung's studio; and Barry Schwabsky, for teasing apart the generative contradictions of the artist's practice.

Our profound thanks to Hyung-teh Do, SungEun Kim, and Jaeseok Kim at Gallery Hyundai for their generous collaboration and kind assistance in facilitating an interview with the artist.

Finally, to Bona Yoo and Emilio Steinberger, whose dedication and deep knowledge paved the way for this project: thank you. Your unfailing support has ensured that Chung's contributions to abstract painting can be grasped in their full profundity and power.

Dominique Lévy | Brett Gorvy

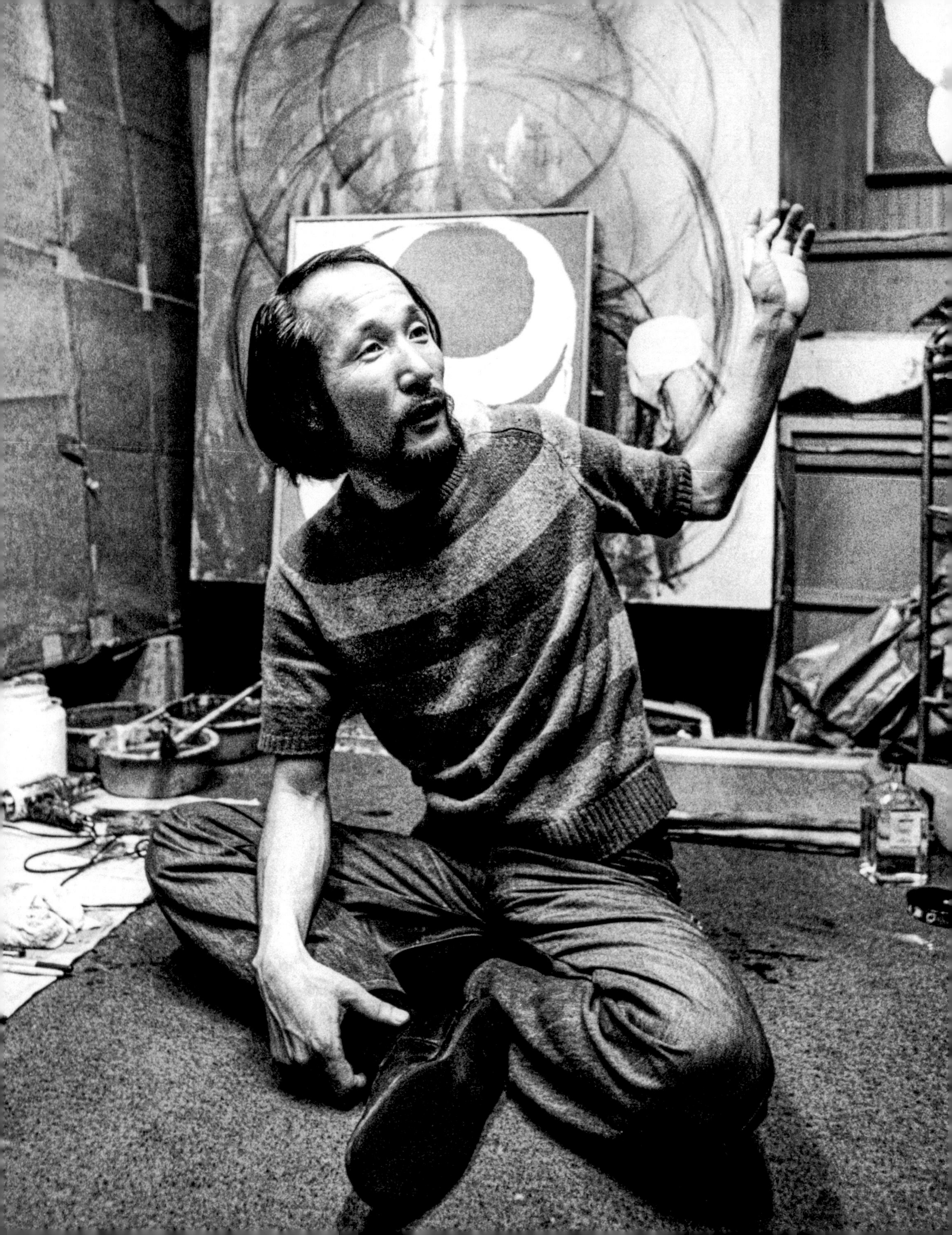

CHUNG SANG-HWA:
POSITIVE PASSIVITY
BARRY SCHWABSKY

Only over the last five years or so has the work of a pioneering generation of South Korean abstract painters—the art that has been popularized under the label *Dansaekhwa*, Korean monochrome—become visible in the United States. Even at home, interest in this work has increased exponentially. But the belated discovery of these artists' work abroad, in particular, should remind us to distrust the fantasy that, in conditions of globalized communications, information spreads almost simultaneously almost everywhere. As a result of this delay in the reception of Korean abstraction, many viewers have little sense of its overall history, not only of the context in which the artists worked and mutually influenced each other but of the vicissitudes of their individual art and its evolution.[1] In many cases, we have become acquainted first with the fully developed work of the artist's later years, with little sense of how they arrived at this mature aesthetic.

In the case of Chung Sang-Hwa, his previous New York showing was a two-gallery affair in 2016, which surveyed his art mainly from the late 1970s—that is, when he was already well into his forties—onward, and included only a couple of earlier paintings. Across four decades of work, one could see Chung tenaciously exploring the many nuances and possibilities of an already well-thought-out approach to painting, to which he has maintained his fidelity through the years. The viewer could easily note the consistency of Chung's choices:

the use in each painting of a single color—occasionally black, more often blue, most often white (a favorite color among many of the artists associated with *Dansaekhwa*)—and a peculiarly subtle tactility in painted surfaces, thanks to the insistently reiterative process by which he made them, which Tim Griffin has explained in a clear, concise way:

> Chung first lays down a mixture of kaolin clay, water, and glue on stretched canvas, which, after the material dries, he unmounts in order to draw grids of lines on its reverse side. Next, the artist folds the canvas and tears off the dried "paint" in strips and squares, before filling in these negative areas with acrylic. Finally, he begins the process all over again and, crucially, repeats it numerous times in turn.[2]

As Griffin noted, this is a process that encompasses all sorts of dualities—making and unmaking, adding and removing, preservation and destruction. Perhaps most important, it creates a dialogue between order and rationality, as embodied in the grid, and randomness or accident, evident in the many small, seemingly insignificant irregularities in the way the innumerable small units fit into the grid structure. Each unit seems to have its own life, its own identity, without contradicting the sense of the whole. One might speak of the creative intention of the artist as he imposes his will—even violently—on his materials, and a kind of quietism in which he allows the material to follow its own nature as the paint fills the spaces and channels he has prepared for it. Although Chung's paintings never involve the kind of mediated "touch" or handwriting that is available to an artist who applies paint to the canvas with a brush, the variability of his painted surfaces lends his works a distinct warmth, a sense of quietly pulsating energy that is organic, not mechanical. That leads to another of the work's embodied dualities: it feels objective but not impersonal, inexpressive yet saturated with humanity.

How does Chung's work contain these apparent contradictions? My way of understanding it comes from what might be an unexpected source. In his essay "The Ruin," the German sociologist and philosopher Georg Simmel points out that in architecture, ruins are inherently meaningful and significant. "The ruin," he said, "means that where the work of art is dying, other forces and forms, those of nature, have grown; and that out of what of art still lives in the ruin and what of nature already lives in it, there has emerged a new whole, a characteristic unity."[3] Nature undoes the work of humans, their impulse to construct, but this happens because "men *let it decay*," and this amounts to "a positive passivity, whereby man makes himself the accomplice of nature."[4] As a result, Simmel continues, "the work of man appears to us entirely as a product of nature. The same forces which give a mountain its shape through weathering, erosion, faulting, growth of vegetation, here do their work on old walls…. Nature has transformed the work of art into

material for her own expression, as she had previously served as material for art."[5] Here, I cannot help but recall Lóránd Hegyi's observation that the surfaces of Chung's paintings, "in their apparently unintentional, objective indifference… are akin to natural objects, such as dry earth, dry riverbeds, cliffs or old walls, rocks or tree trunks transformed by slow erosion."[6] These paintings do not represent nature, and yet they present themselves as fundamentally akin to the products of nature—even while we see them, framed rectangles on a wall, as quintessentially products of art, of culture.

Simmel was writing in 1911. What he could not have foreseen was that in the century to follow, artists would increasingly come to actively seek out this collaboration with the forces of nature—making nature their accomplice as well as becoming its accomplice in a new form of creation. John Cage welcomed chance into his compositions. Sol LeWitt declared: "The artist's will is secondary to the process he initiates from idea to completion," so that "the process is carried out blindly," thereby revising the notion of what the completion of an artwork consists of.[7] Lee Ufan, it has been said, "believed that the unmade needed to be introduced" into art, "rather than something that was made."[8] These artists and many more have incorporated into their work something like what Simmel would have seen as its ruin. They make their artistic intentions into material for an expression that is not necessarily their own; their art recedes into what the artists of an earlier time would have dismissed as merely effects of nature rather than art—which had been seen, at least in the West, as a conquest of nature. They deliberately employ what Simmel referred to as "positive passivity."

Like many of his South Korean colleagues, Chung too has endeavored to incorporate ruin and destruction—the unmade—into his artistic process. The present selection of works, which samples his paintings from 1964 through 1978, gives us greater insight into how he arrived at his mature method. With fluid forms unrestricted by the grid, much of this work is distinct in appearance from what his art eventually became. Yet this selection reveals what had long been true of his work: the tropism toward a violation of the physical integrity of the materials. Thanks to Chung's use of kaolin in his paintings of the 1960s and early 1970s—as it would be again later on—the edges of the forms we see in them always discreetly display their status as broken. "More than any of his contemporaries, Chung quickly understood that Korean Informel was doomed by its apparent refusal to give up the idea that surfaces must always be solid and resistant. He grabbed portions of stretched canvas and sometimes twisted them to create whorls," Joan Kee observed. "To disrupt the canvas further, he occasionally thrust his knee against the surface from behind, forcing it to protrude. No longer was it necessary to paint as if the support was always tough, unyielding, and stationary."[9] To those observations I would add that Chung's "tough love" for the painting-object bespeaks an underlying confidence in its fundamental durability—what Lee Yil called "a sense of resilient existence."[10] One senses in Chung's work a faith that even an extreme degree of mistreatment may elicit otherwise unknown and unknowable potential latent within the painting-object—and that this durability is underwritten by an agreement between artistic will and the natural tendency of materials, a nature that things and people inherently share.

NOTES

1. For an overview of Korean abstraction, the basic work in English is the impressive book by Joan Kee, *Contemporary Korean Art: Tansaekhwa and the Urgency of Method* (Minneapolis: University of Minnesota Press, 2013). Also available in English, in a series sponsored by AICA, the International Association of Art Critics: a selection of writings by the prominent South Korean art critic Lee Yil, *Dynamics of Expansion and Reduction—Selected Writings on Korean Contemporary Art*, Chung Yeon Shim and Jean-Marc Poinsot, eds. (Dijon: Les presses du réel, 2018).

2. Tim Griffin, "Time and Again: The Process of Chung Sang-Hwa," in *Chung Sang-Hwa* (New York: Dominique Lévy/Greene Naftali, 2016), 11–12.

3. Georg Simmel, "The Ruin," transl. David Kettler, *The Hudson Review* vol. 11 no. 3 (Autumn, 1958): 380.

4. Simmel, 380. Italics in translation.

5. Simmel, 381.

6. Lóránd Hegyi, "Chung Sang-Hwa's Pictorial Messages: Perspectives of Internalization—Metaphors of Appropriation," in *Chung Sang-Hwa: Painting Archeology* (Saint-Étienne: Musée d'Art Moderne de Saint-Étienne Métropole, 2011), 18.

7. Sol LeWitt, "Sentences on Conceptual Art," in *Conceptual Art: A Critical Anthology*, Alexander Alberro and Blake Stimson, eds. (Cambridge: MIT Press, 1999), 106, 107.

8. Sook-Kyung Lee, "Man and nature united: In the studio: Lee Ufan," *Tate etc.* 31 (Summer 2014). https://www.tate.org.uk/tate-etc/issue-31-summer-2014/man-and-nature-united

9. Joan Kee, "Tansaekhwa, Inside and Out," in Joan Kee, *From All Sides: Tansaekhwa on Abstraction* (Los Angeles: Blum & Poe, 2015), 11.

10. Lee Yil, "Intimate Space for Breathing: Chung Sang-Hwa's Exhibition, 1980," in *Dynamics of Expansion and Reduction*, 139.

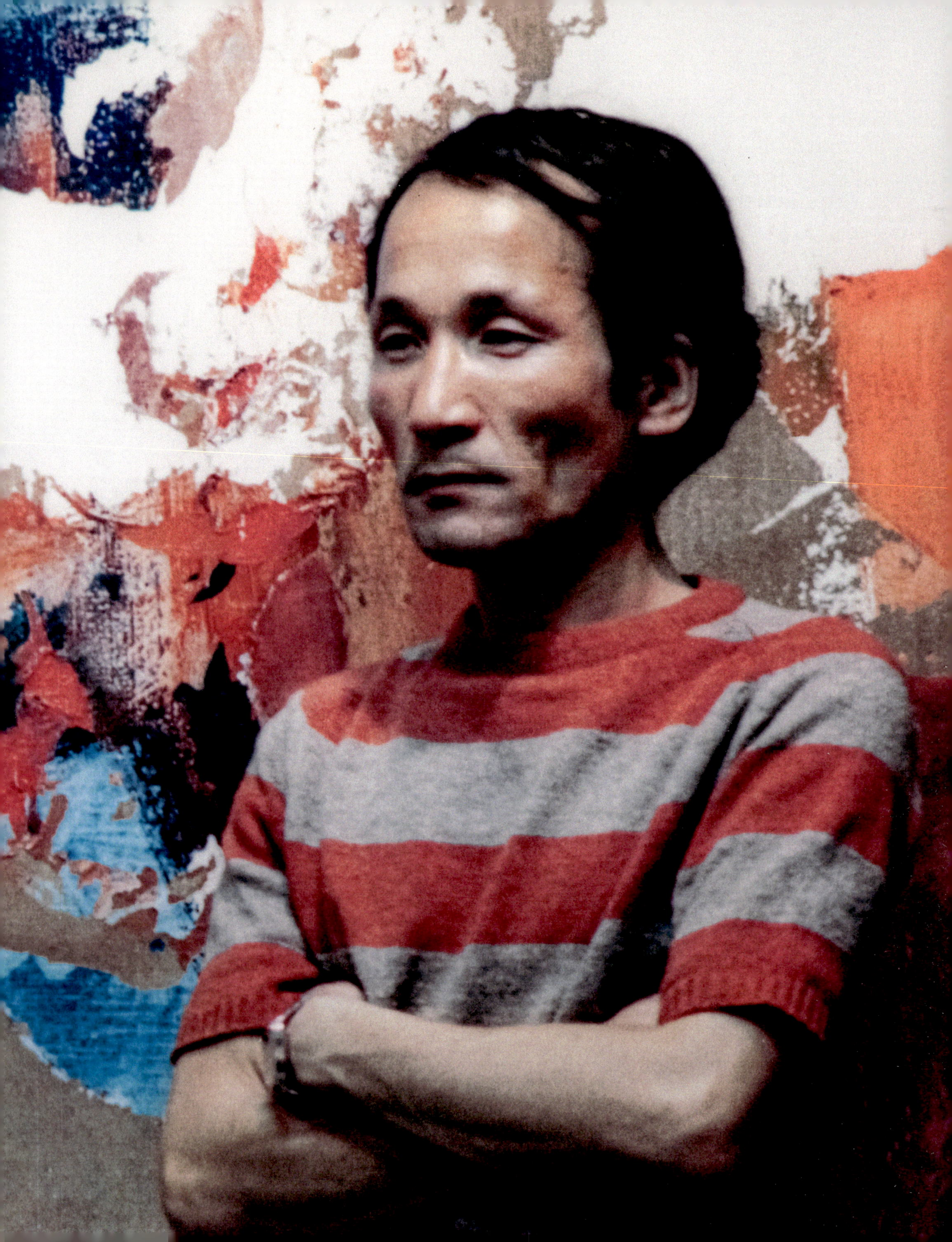

LIKE THE VERY FIRST TIME

Like a young bird encountering the sky for the very first time

Like the sprout pressing down into the earth and then lifting up for the very first time

Even as the day grows dark at evening

Like morning

Like the new spring

Like the very first time

We are beginning a new day.

—Shin Young-Bok

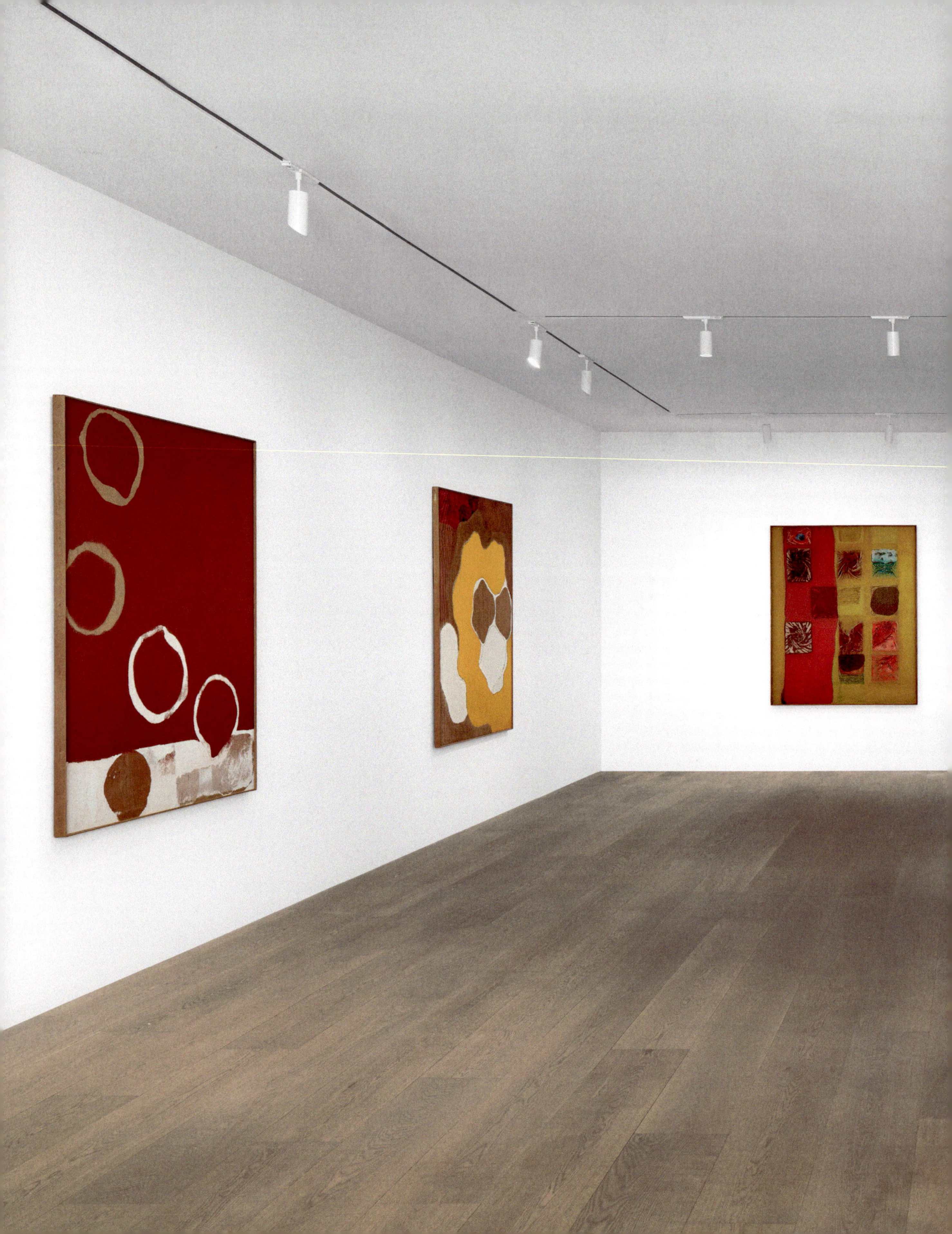

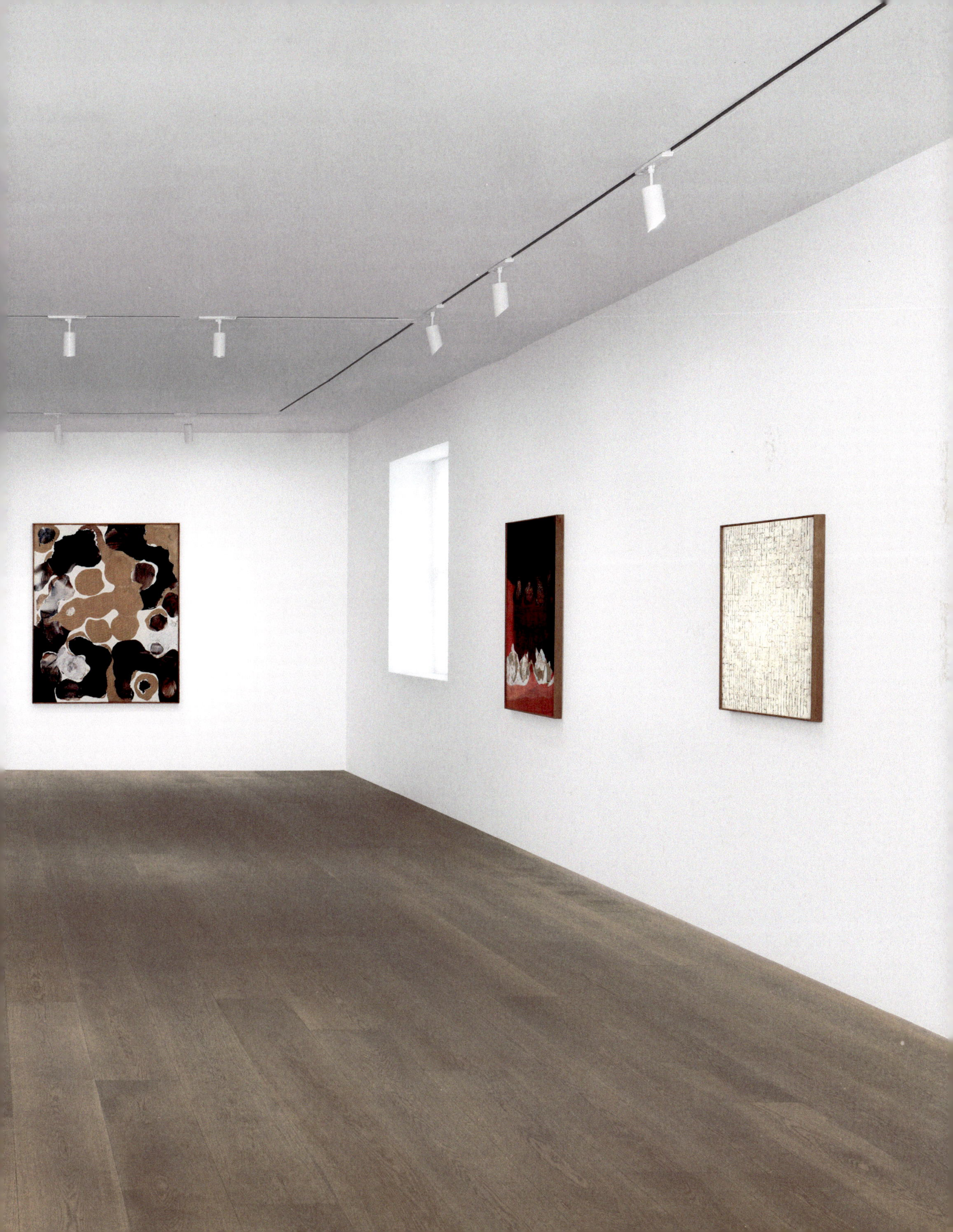

WORK 64-13

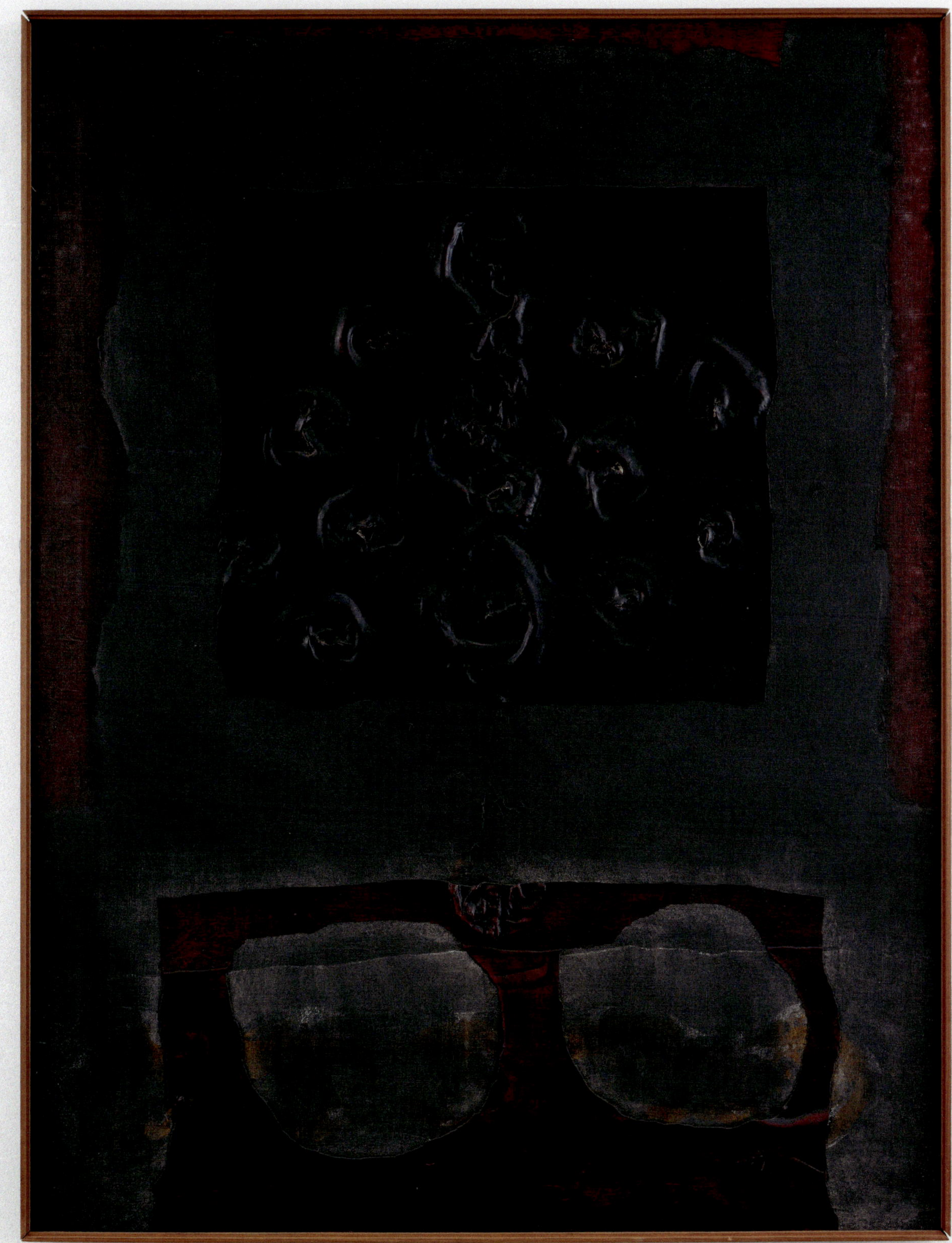

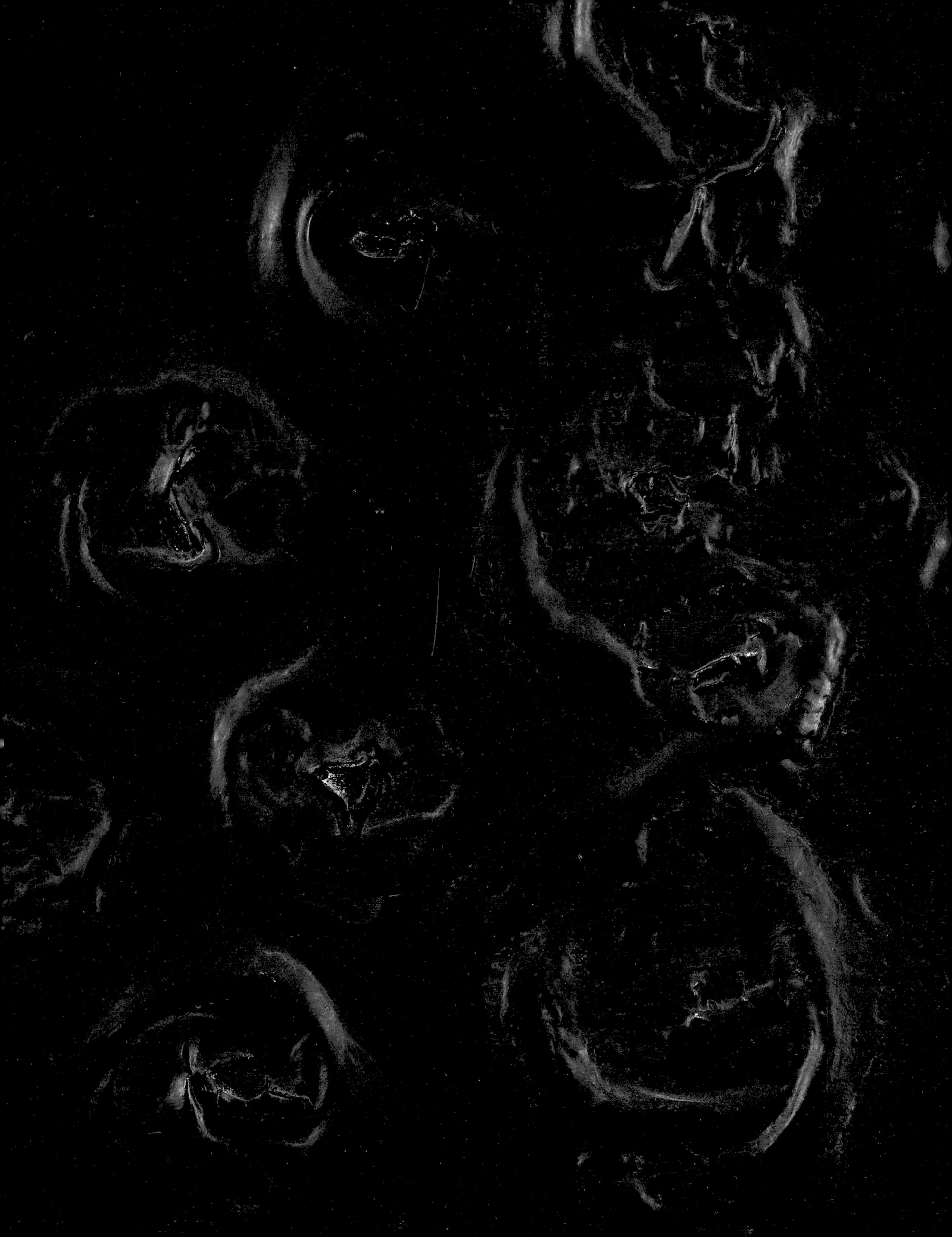

WORK 65-2

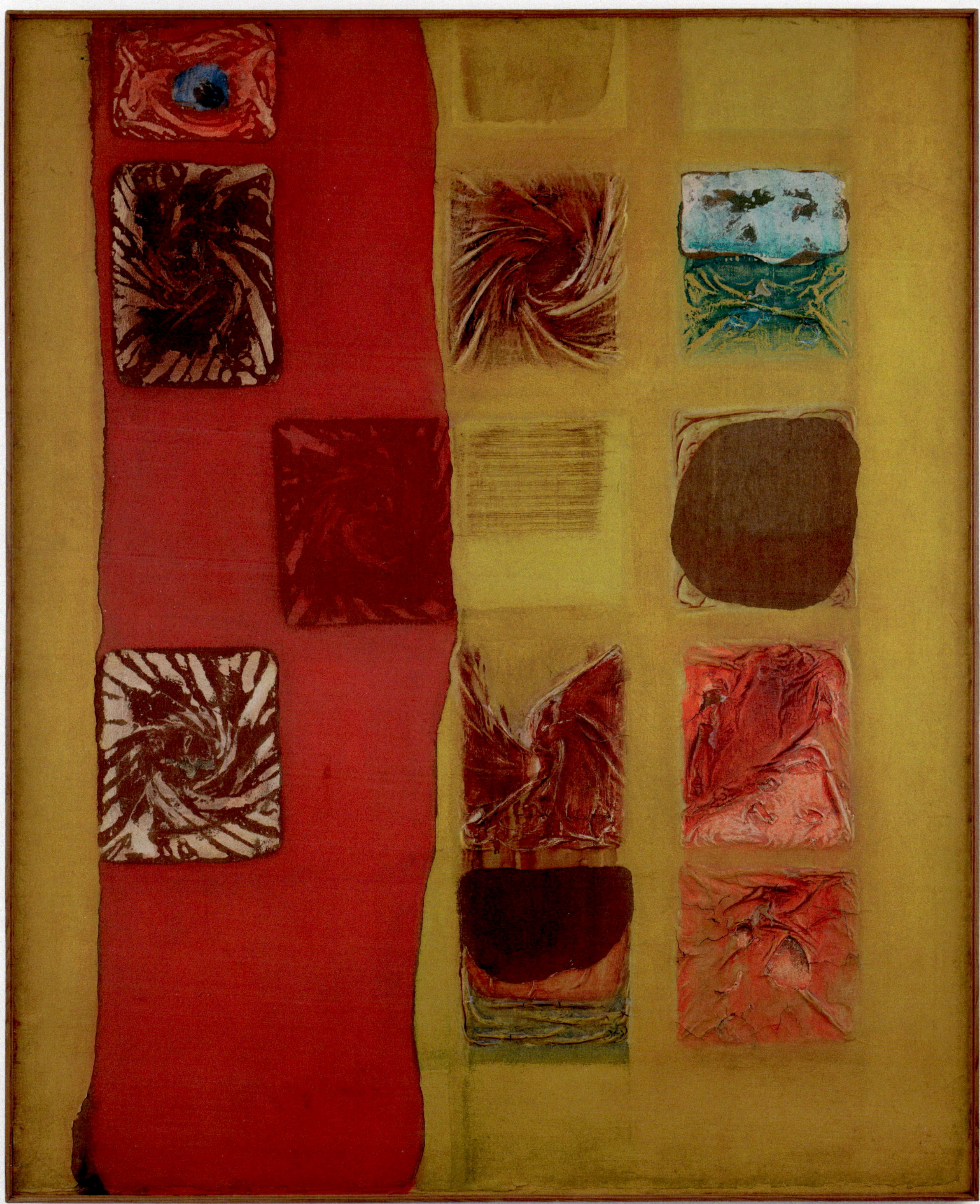

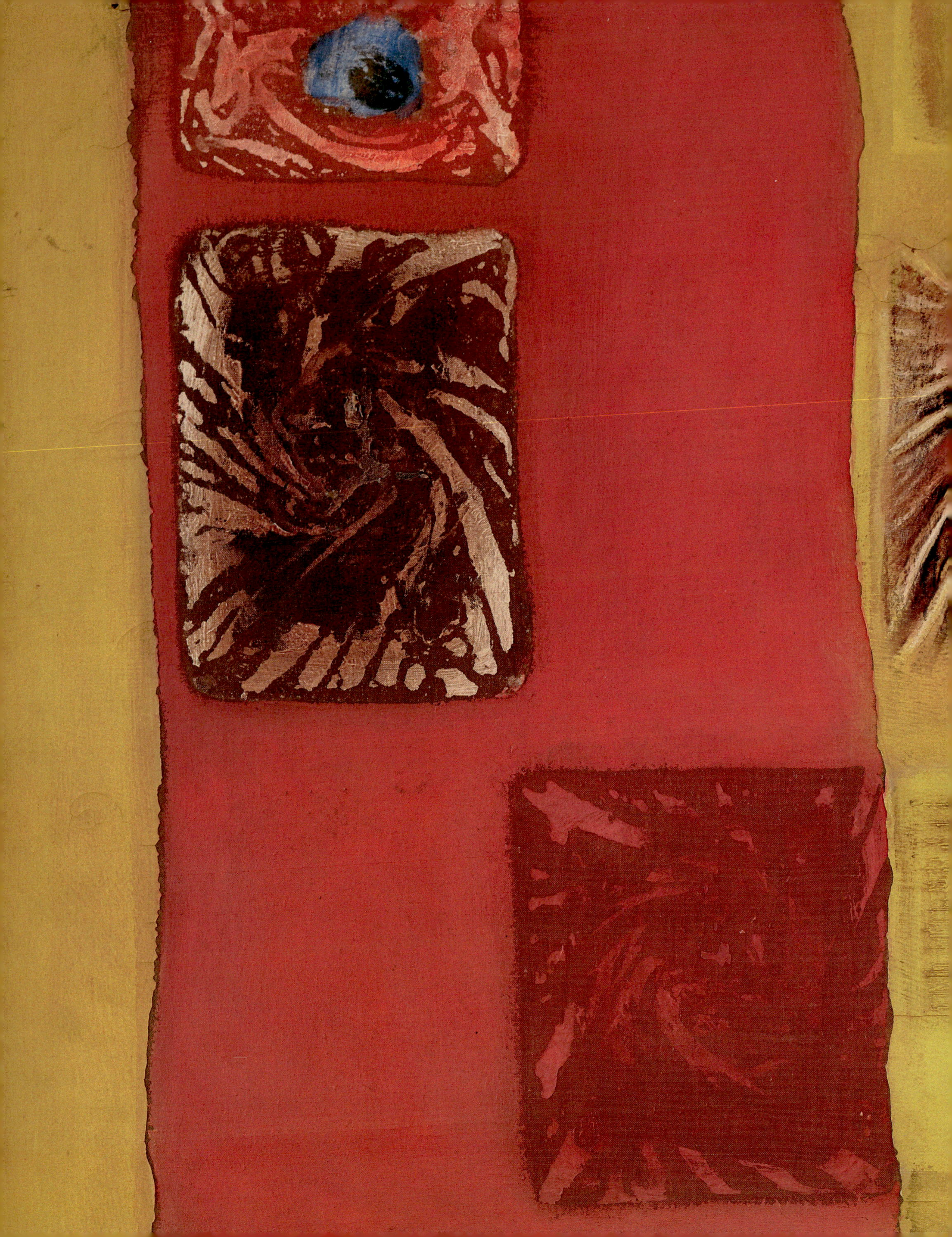

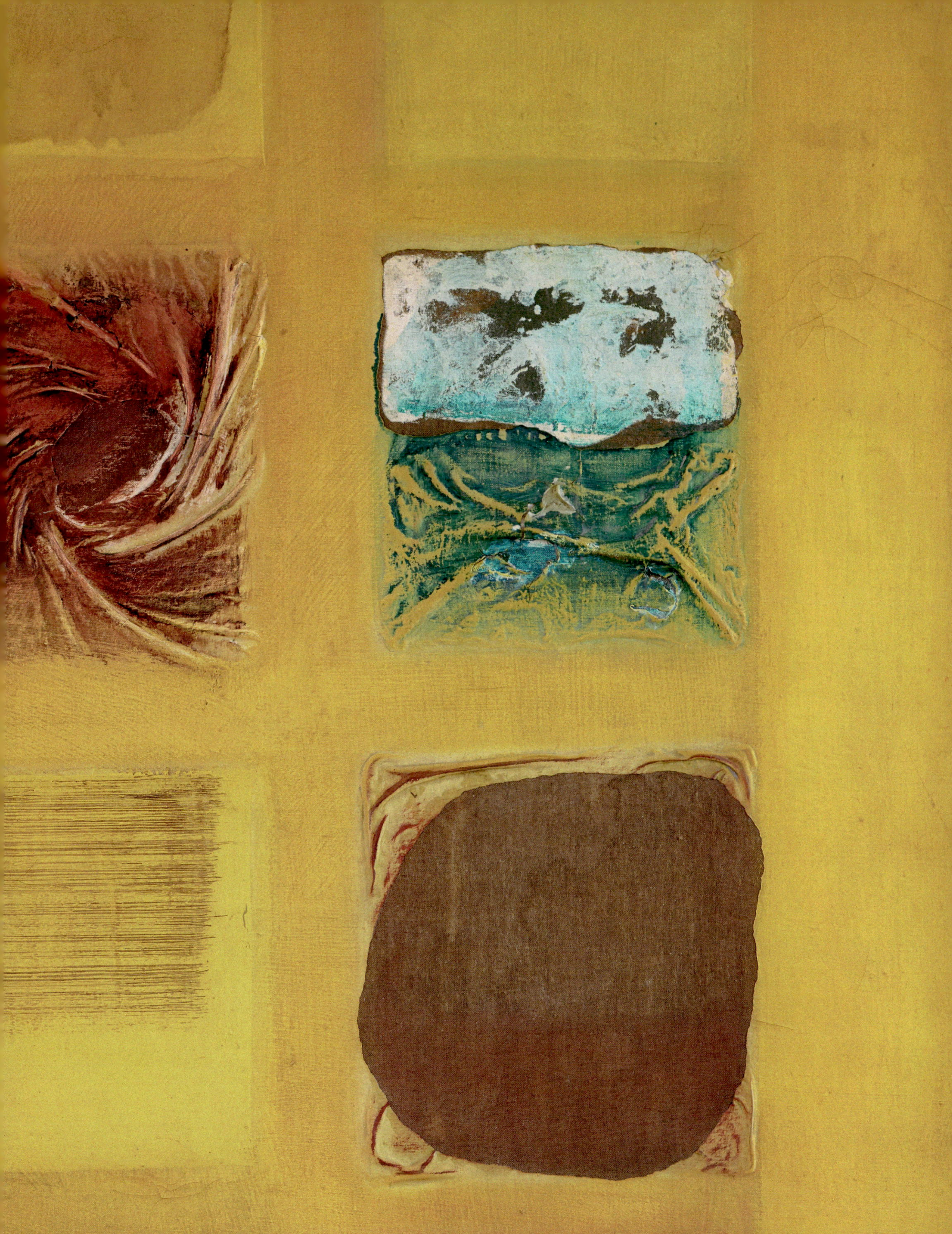

WORK 68-32

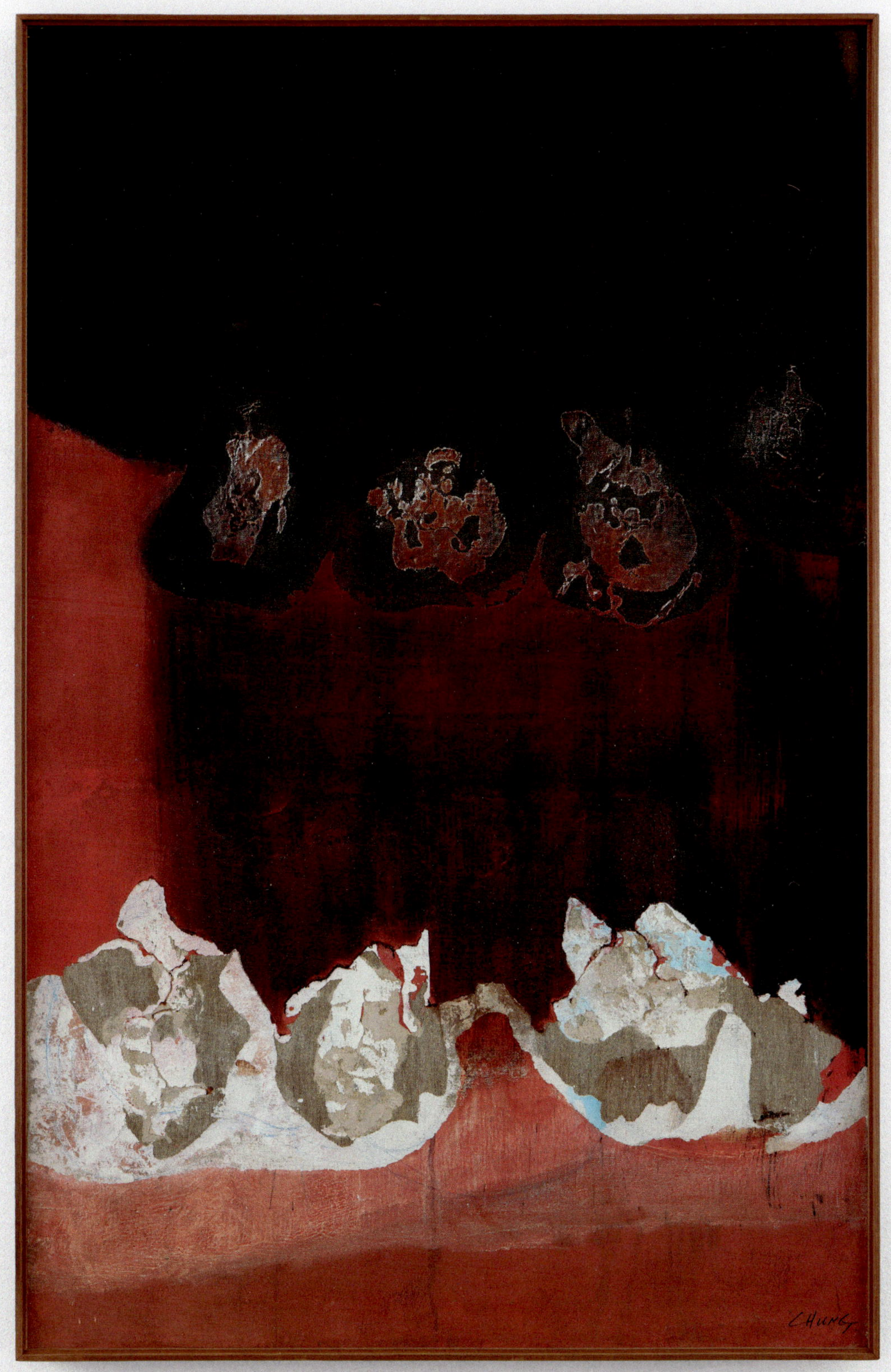

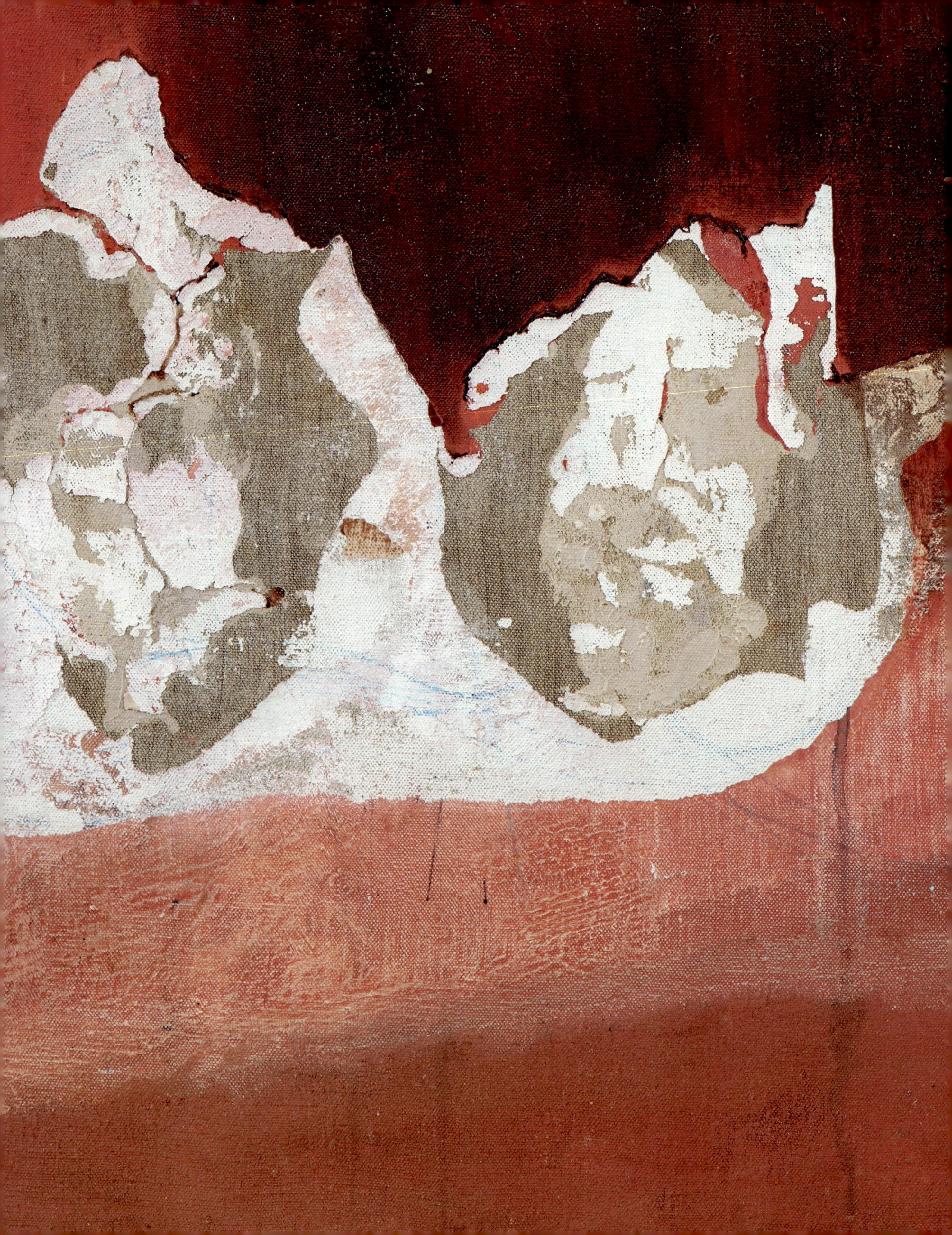

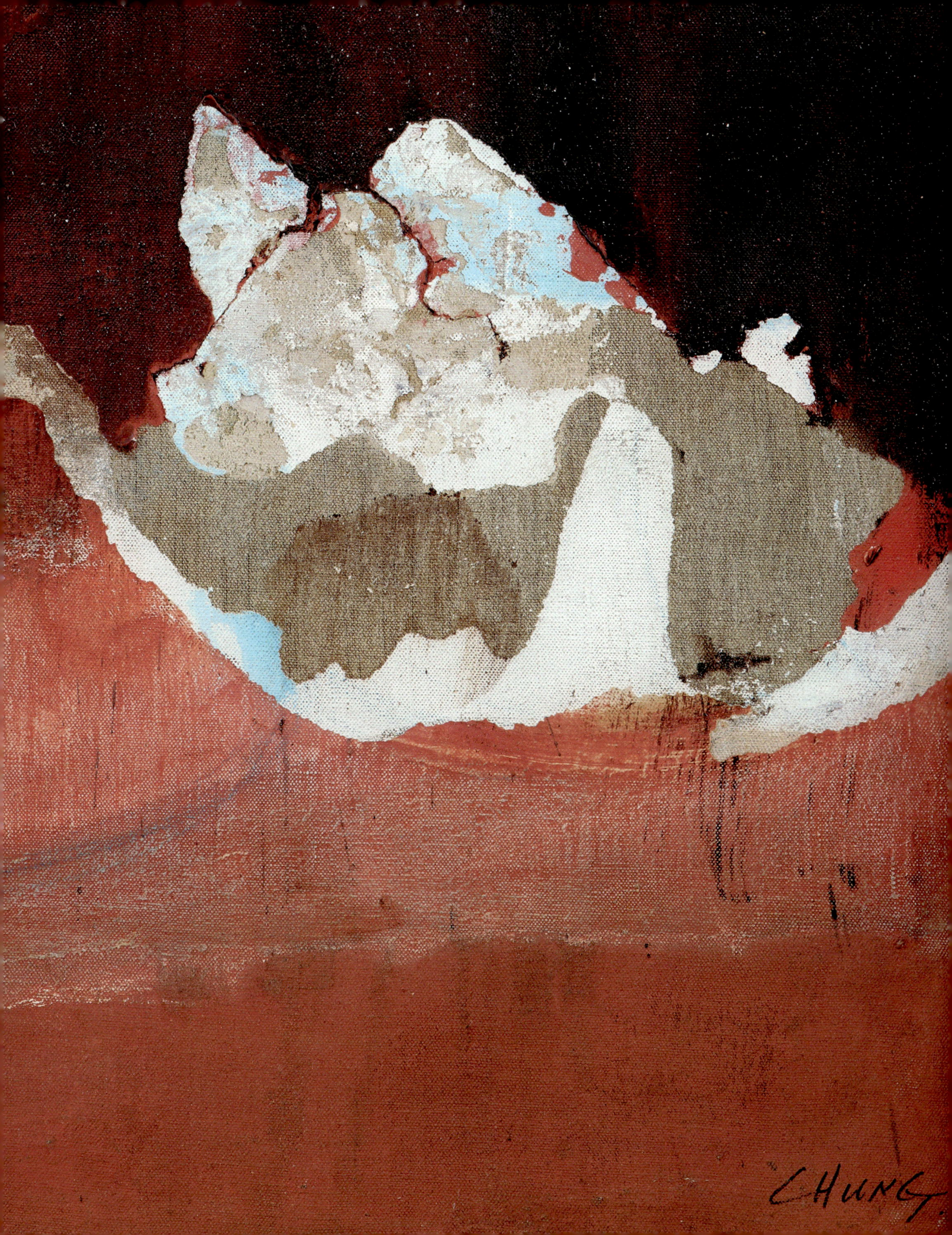

CHUNG

WORK 69-A

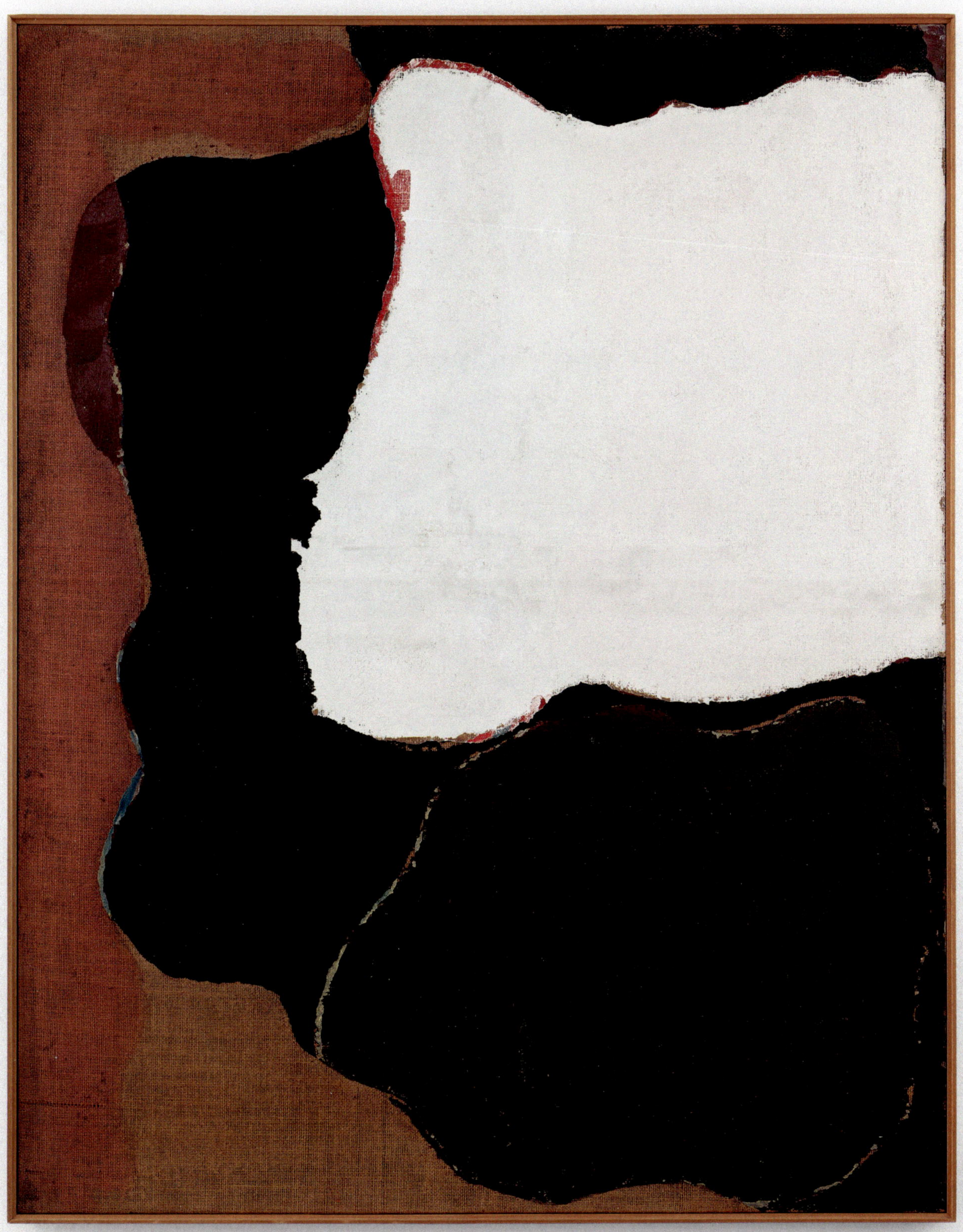

WORK 70-9-15

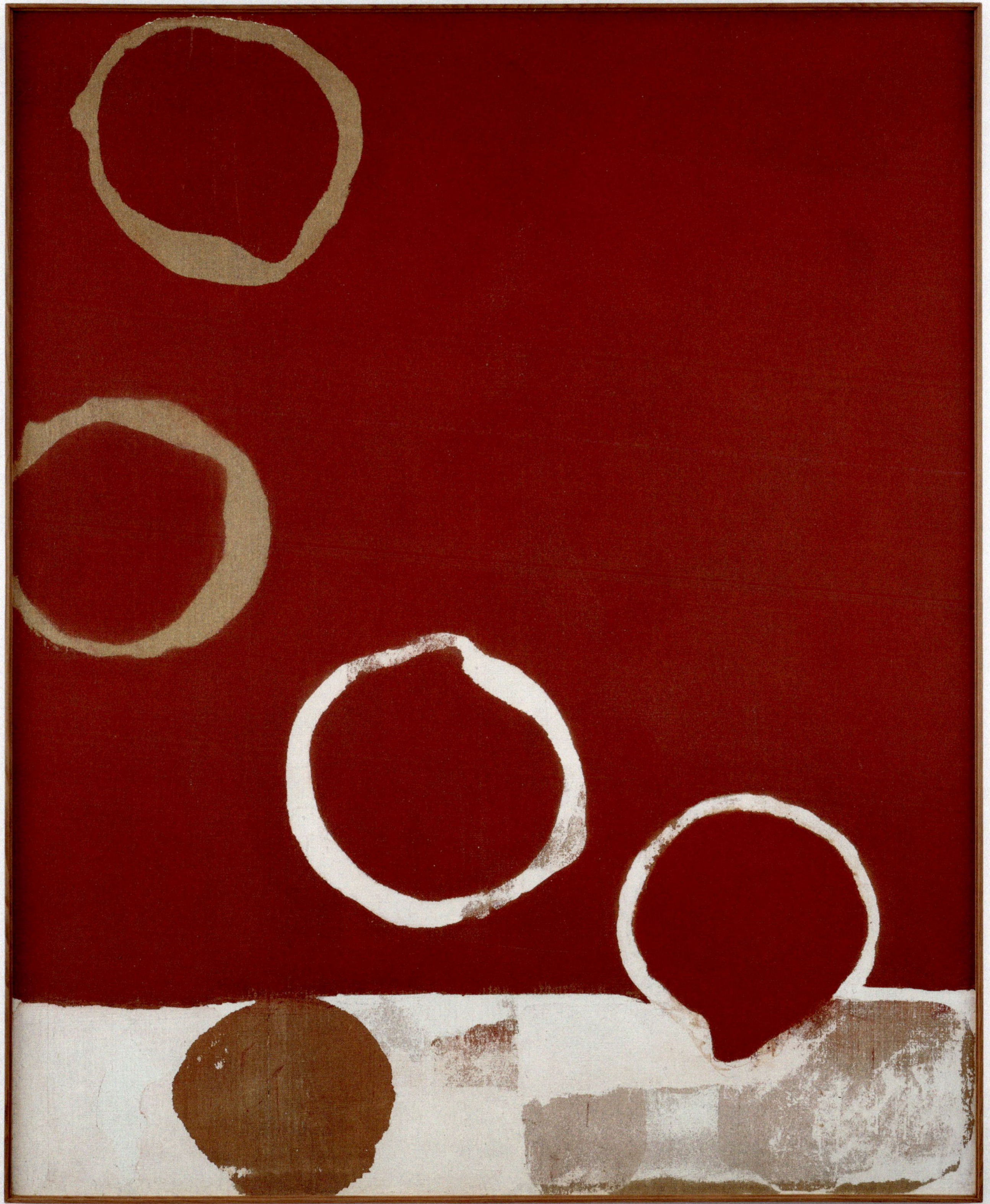

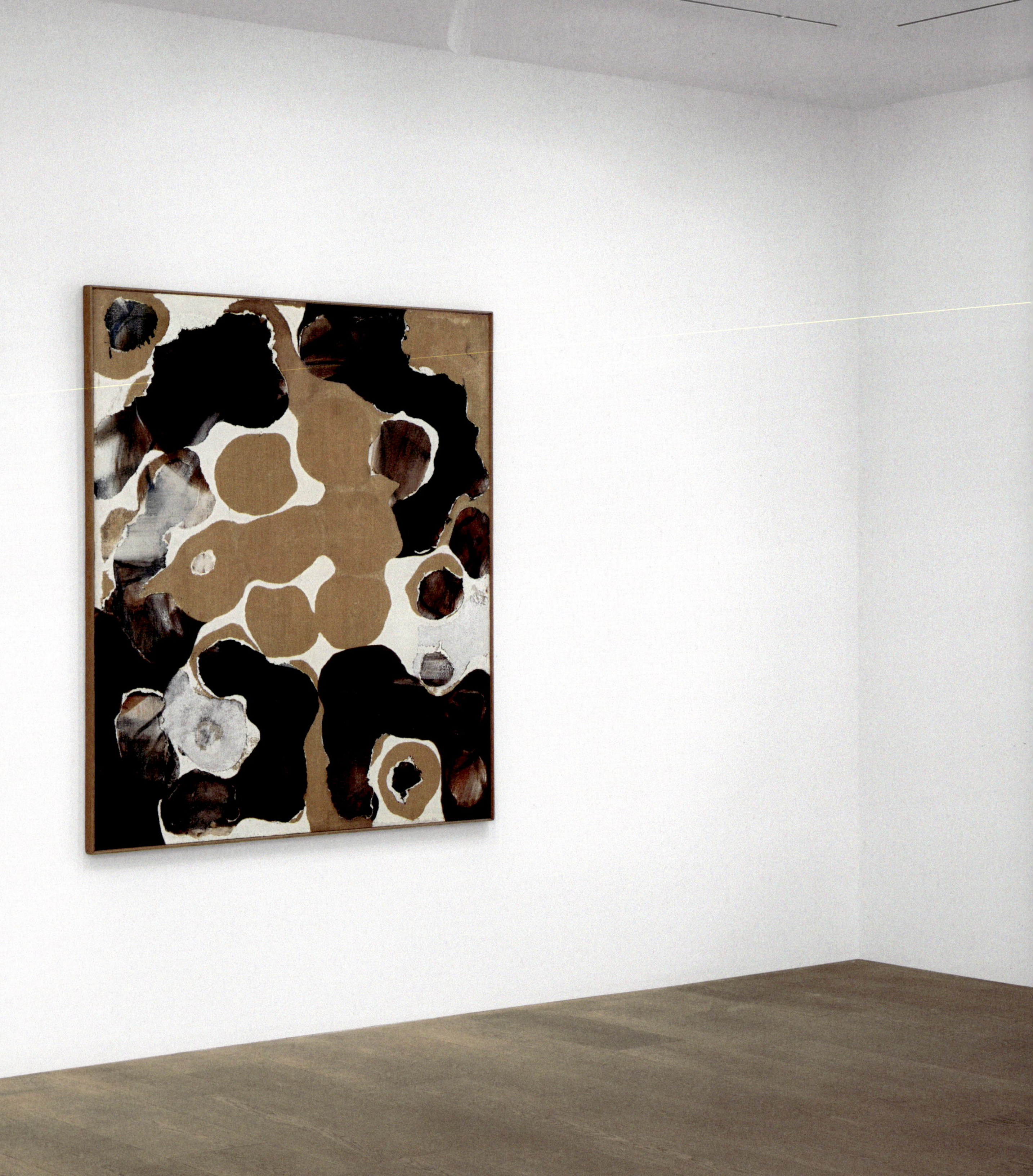

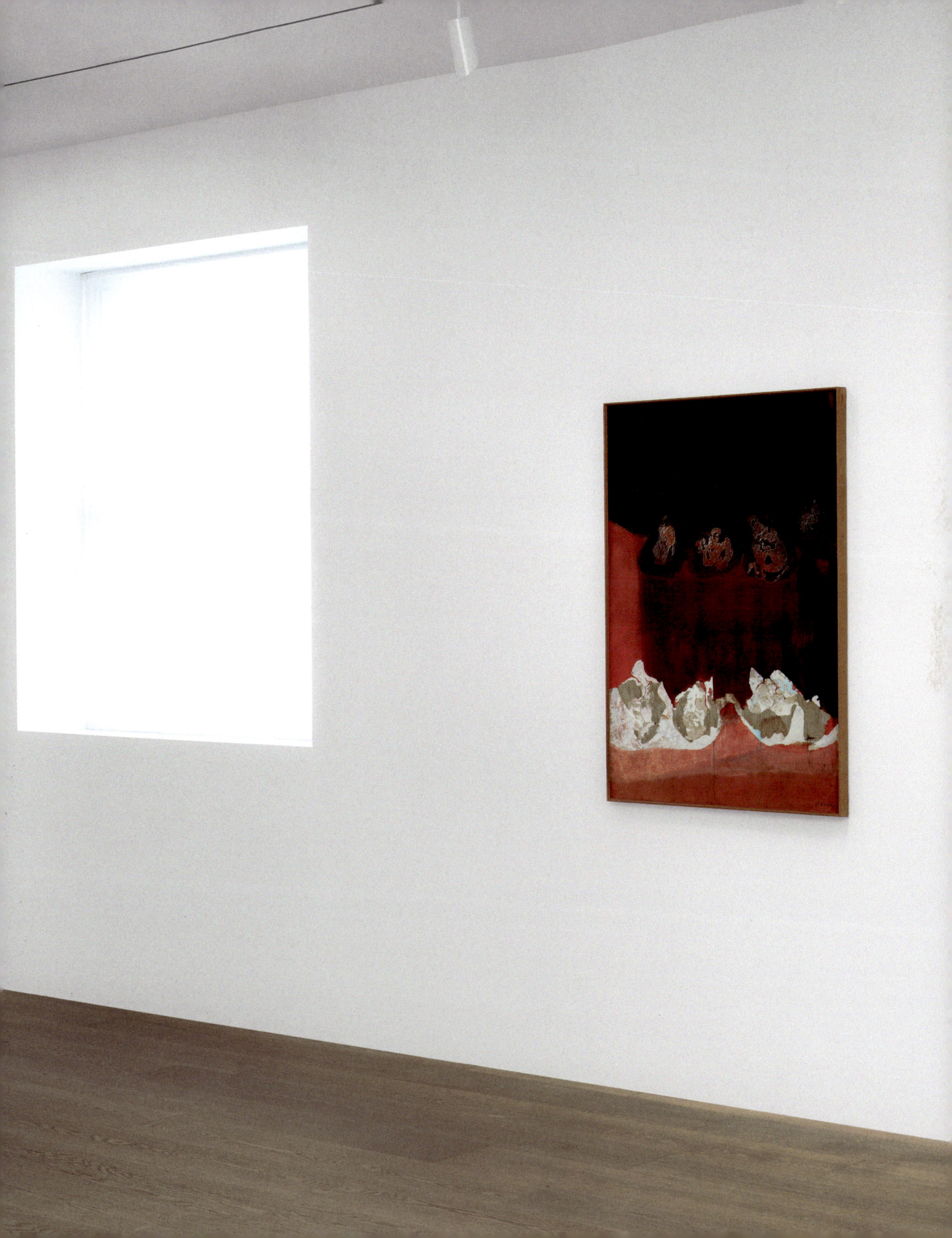

WORK K-3

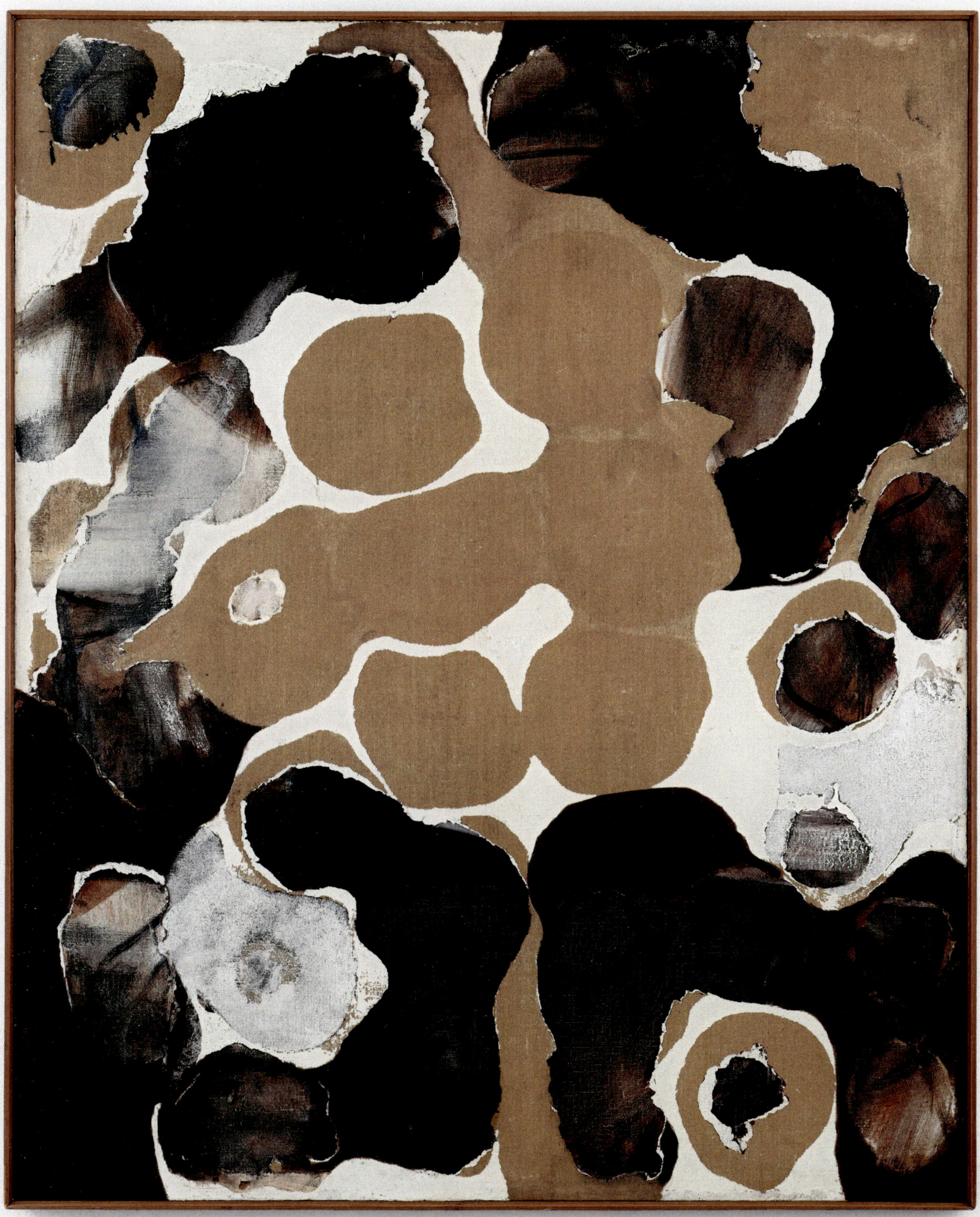

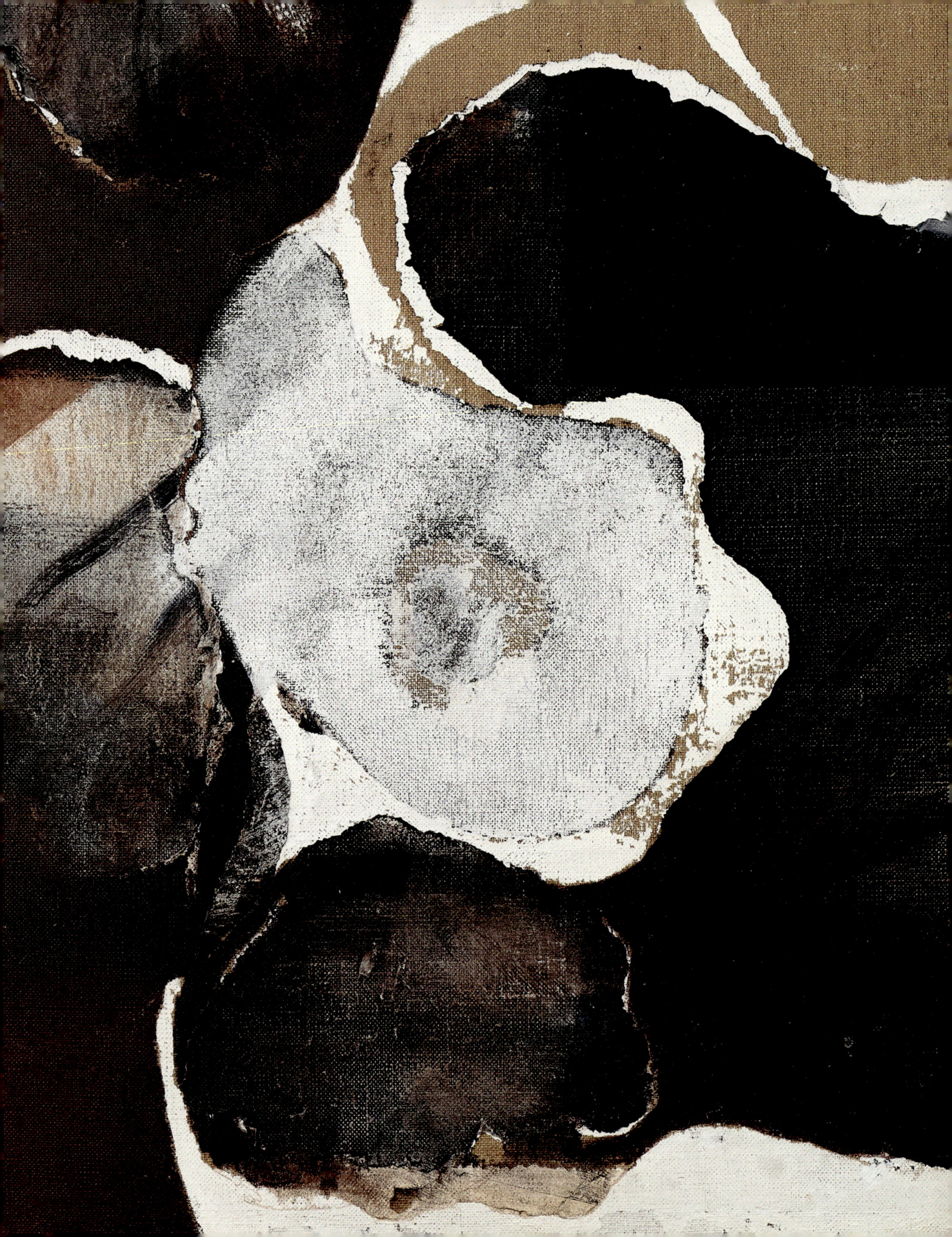

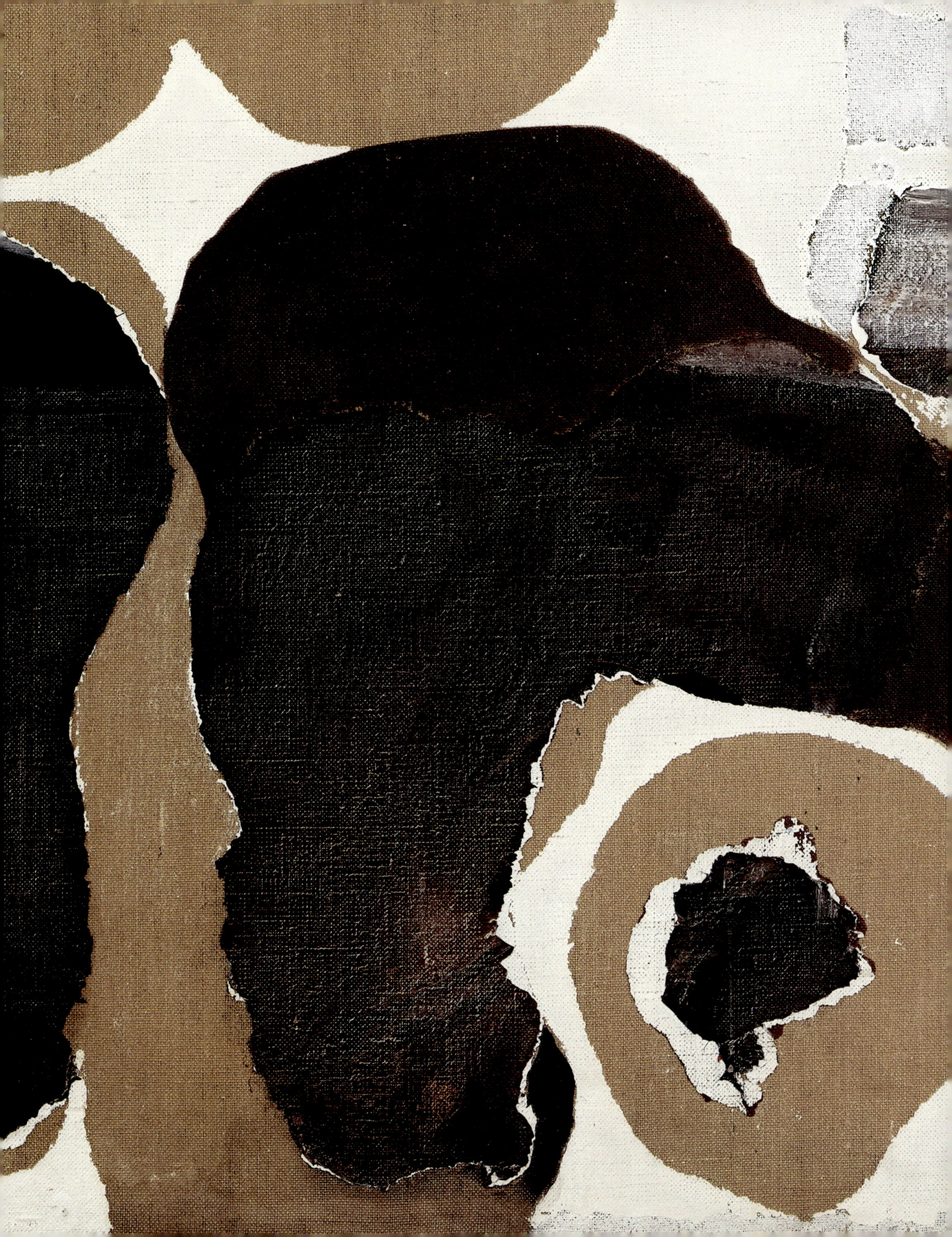

WORK O-A

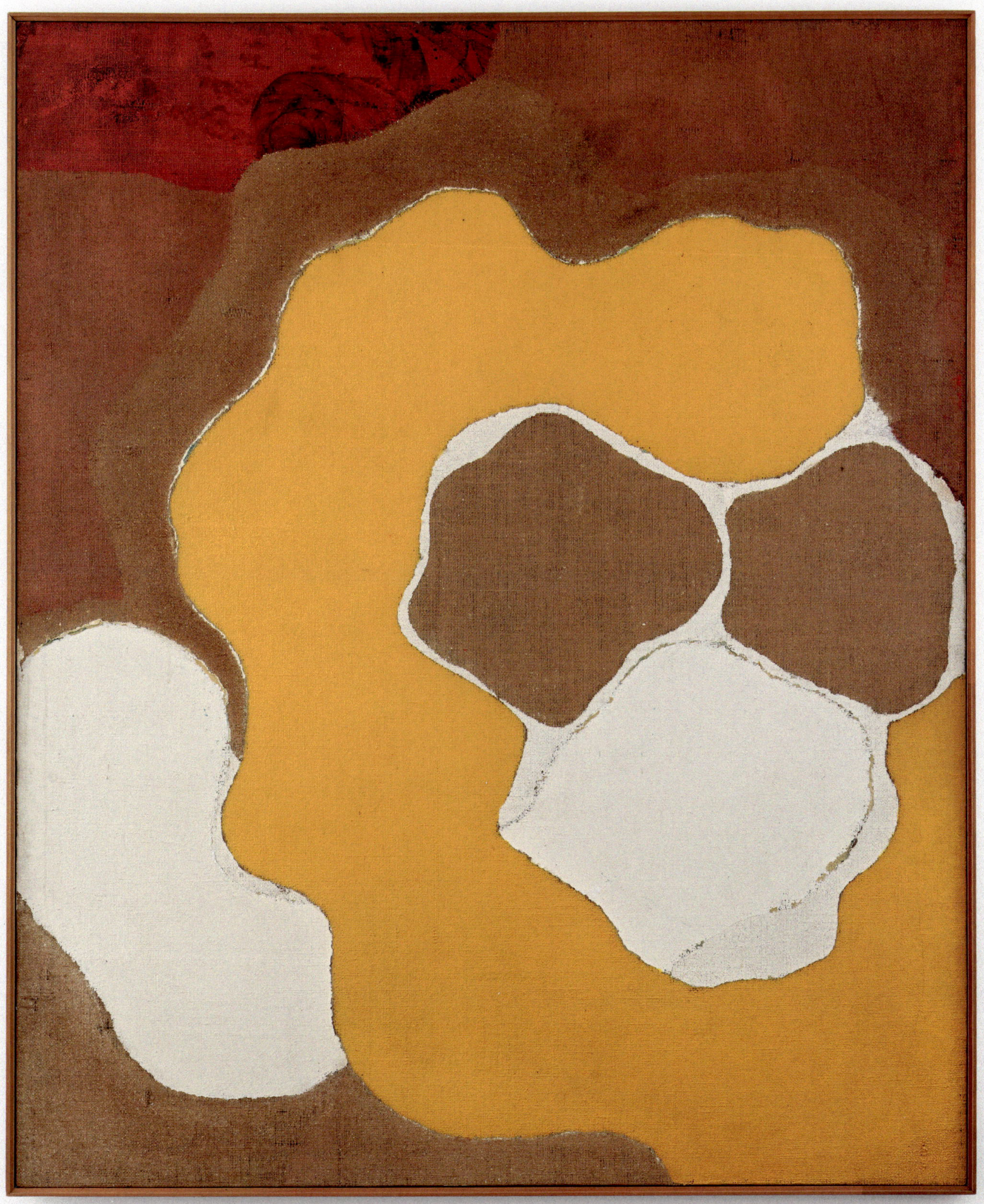

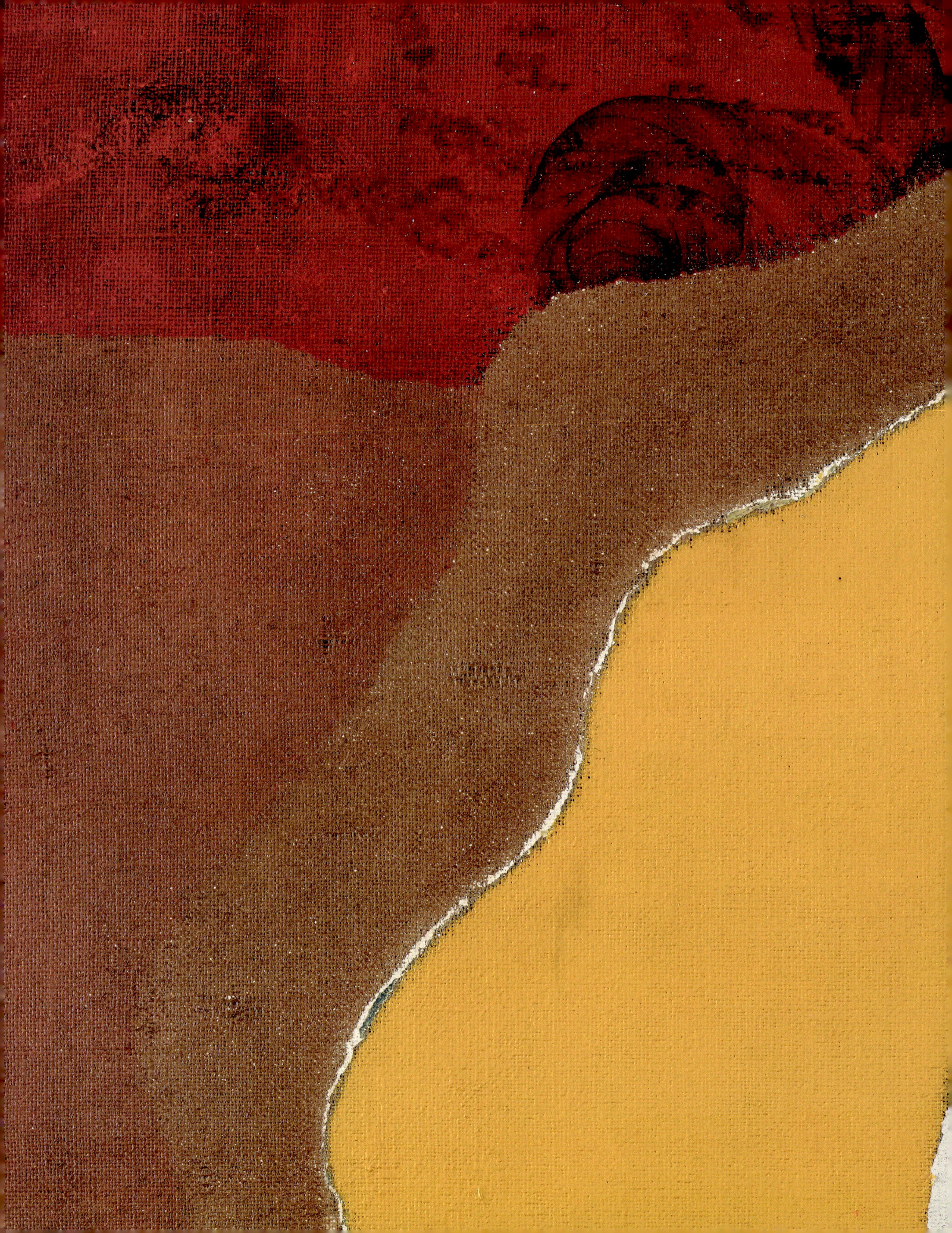

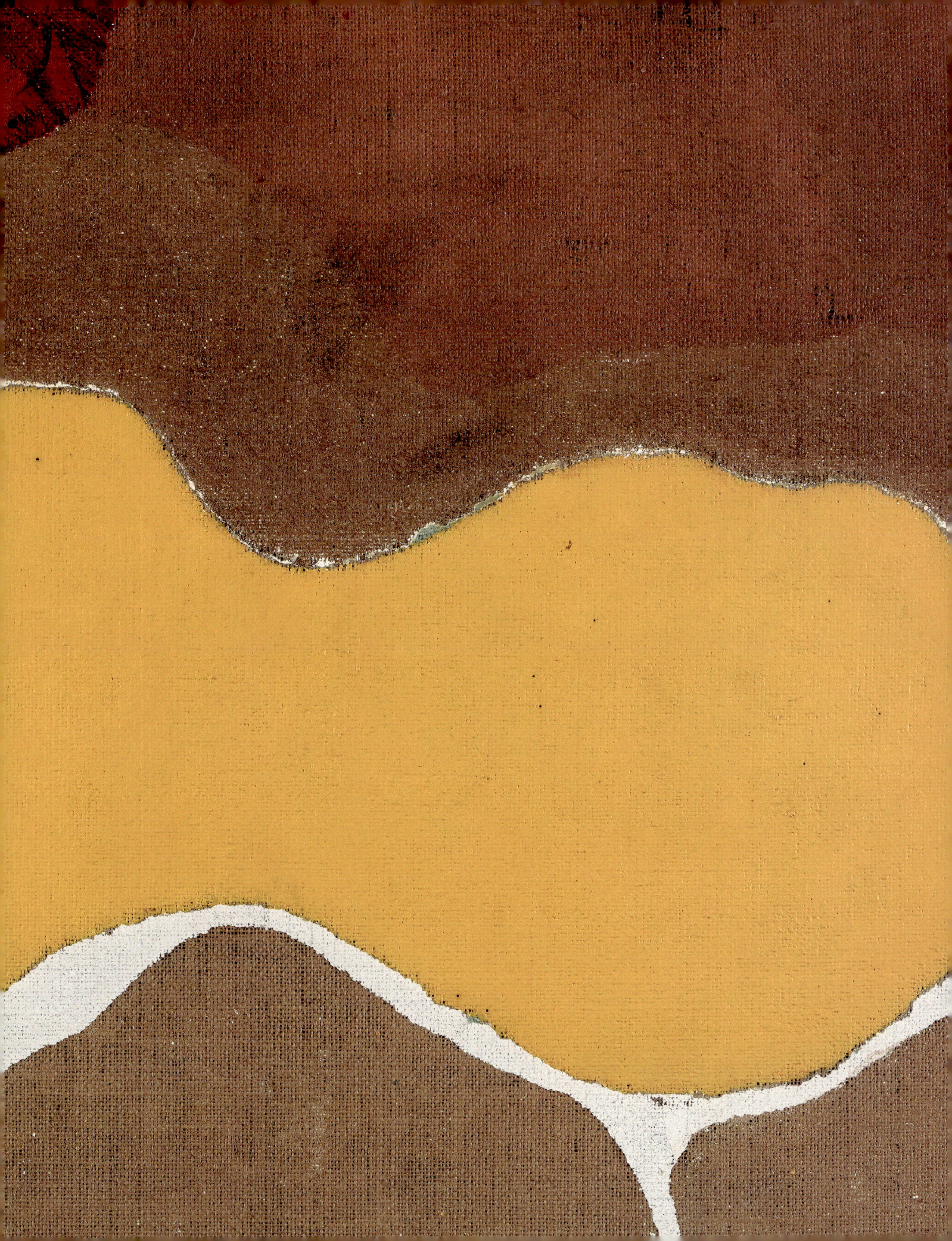

WORK 72-B

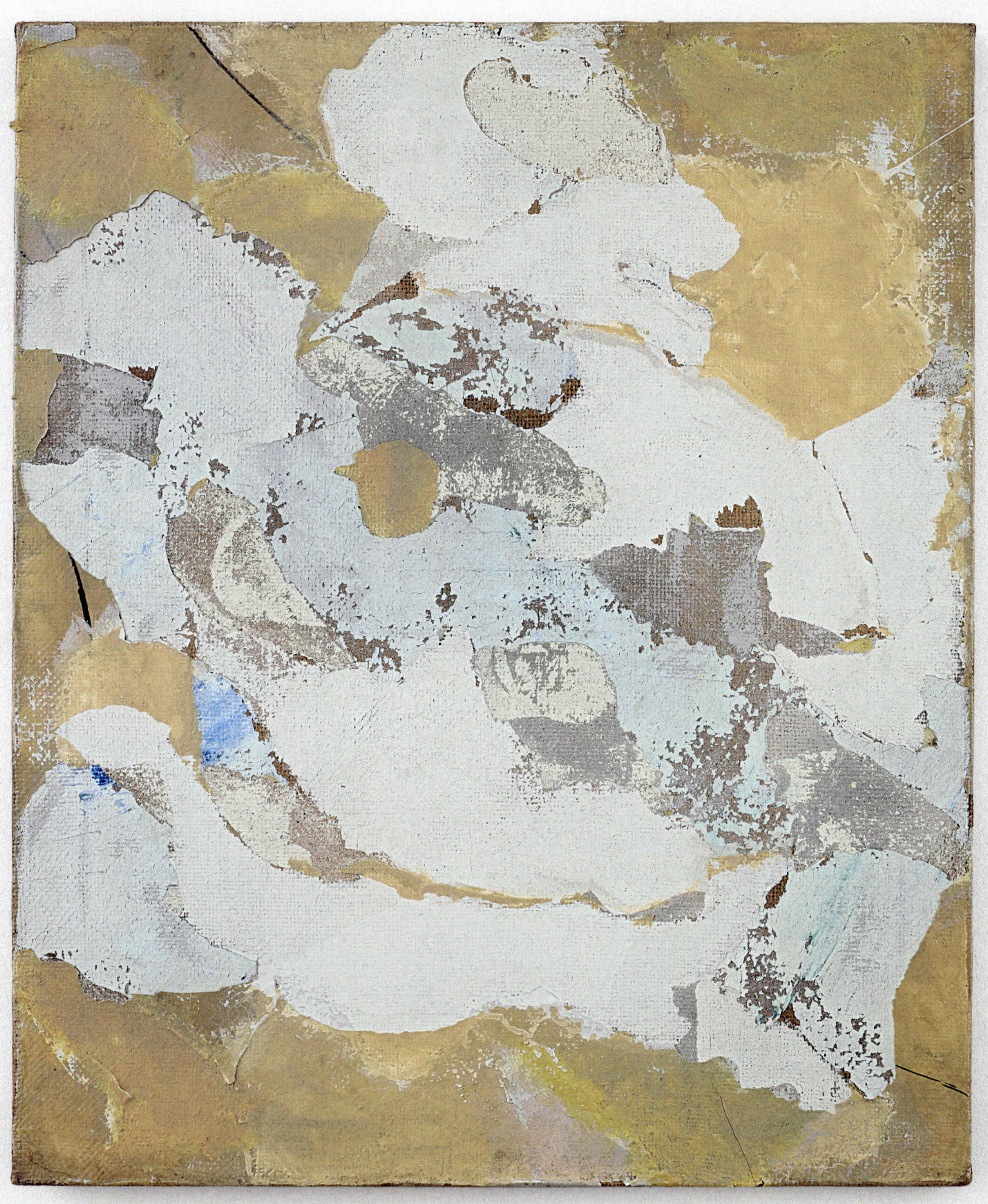

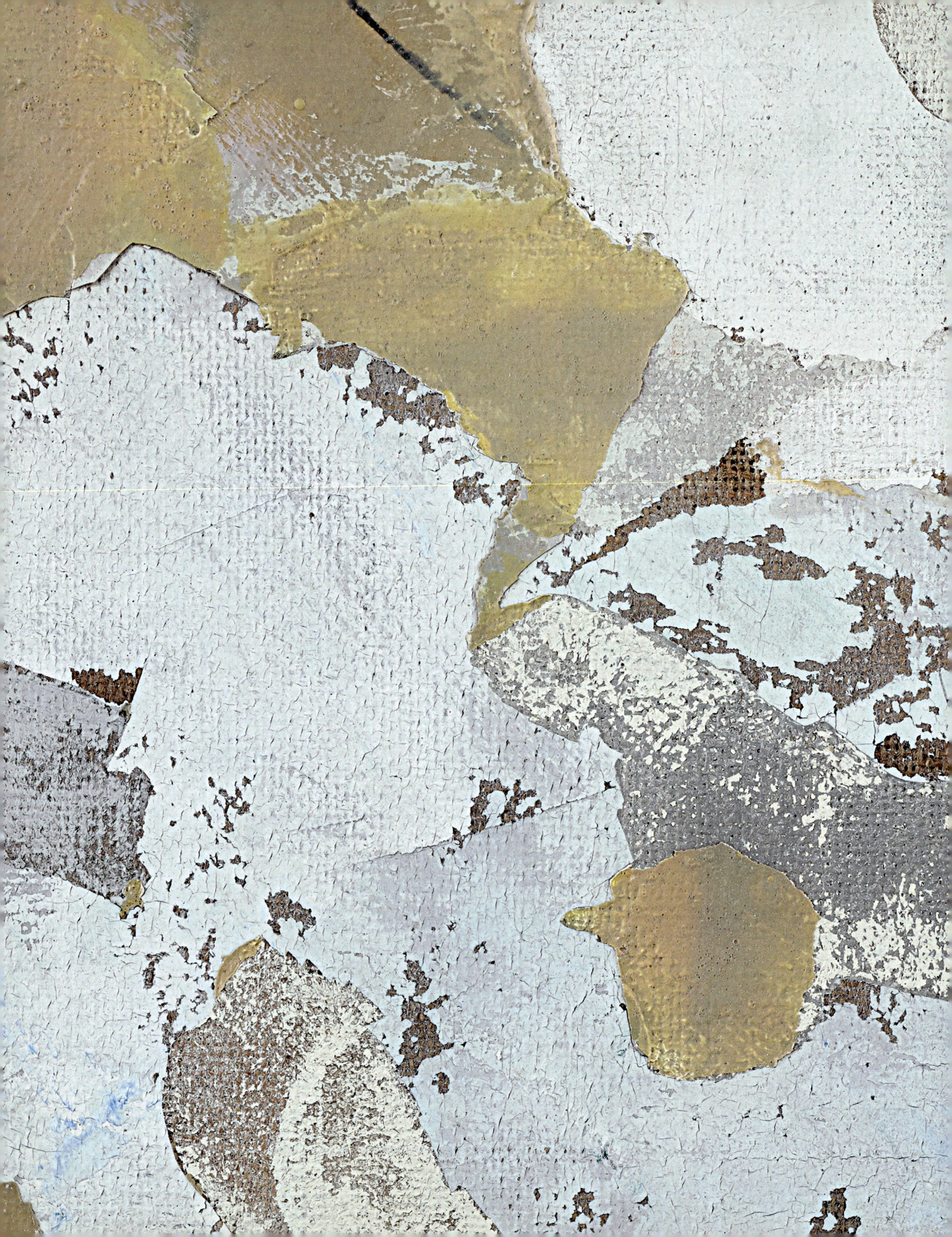

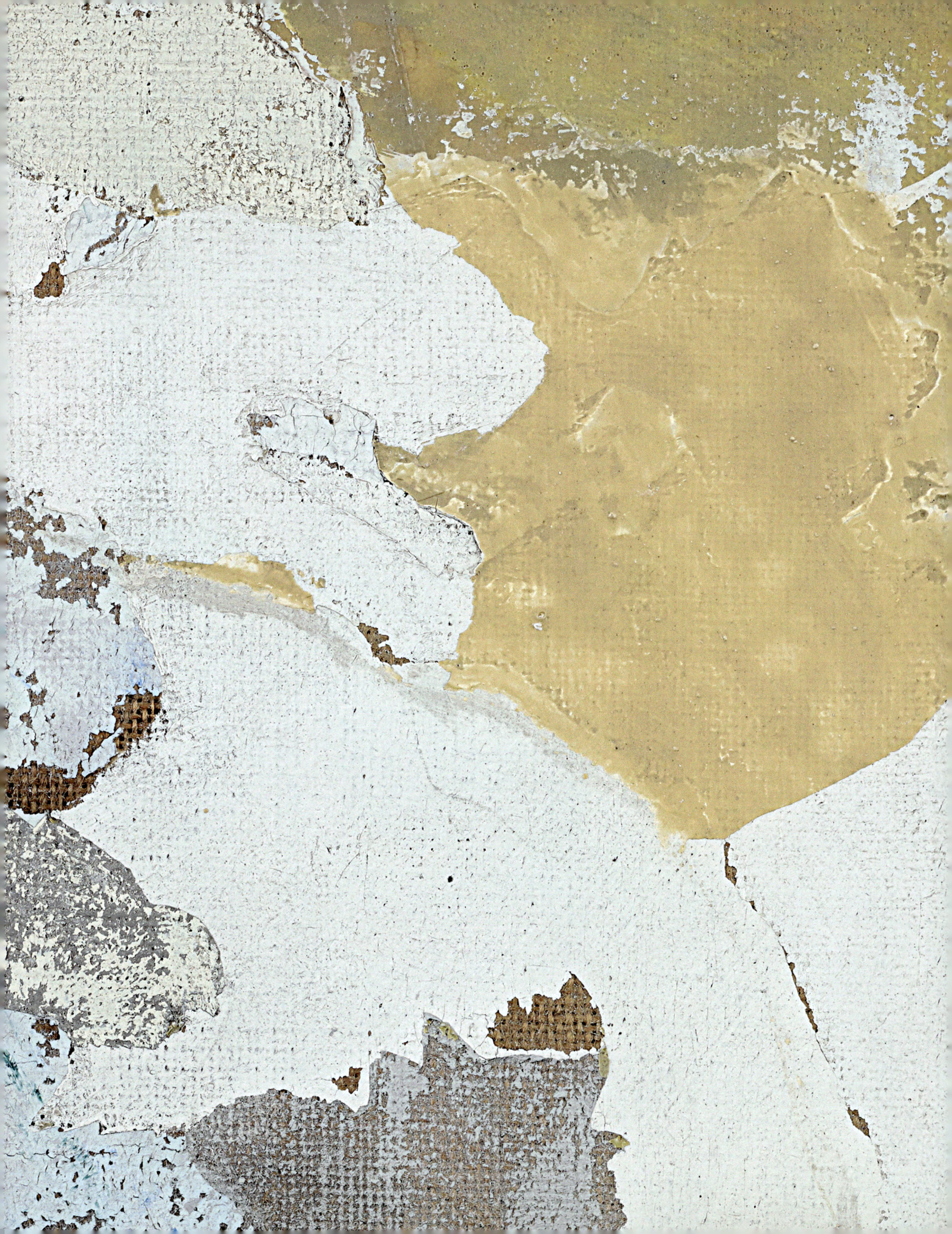

UNTITLED 75-10-8

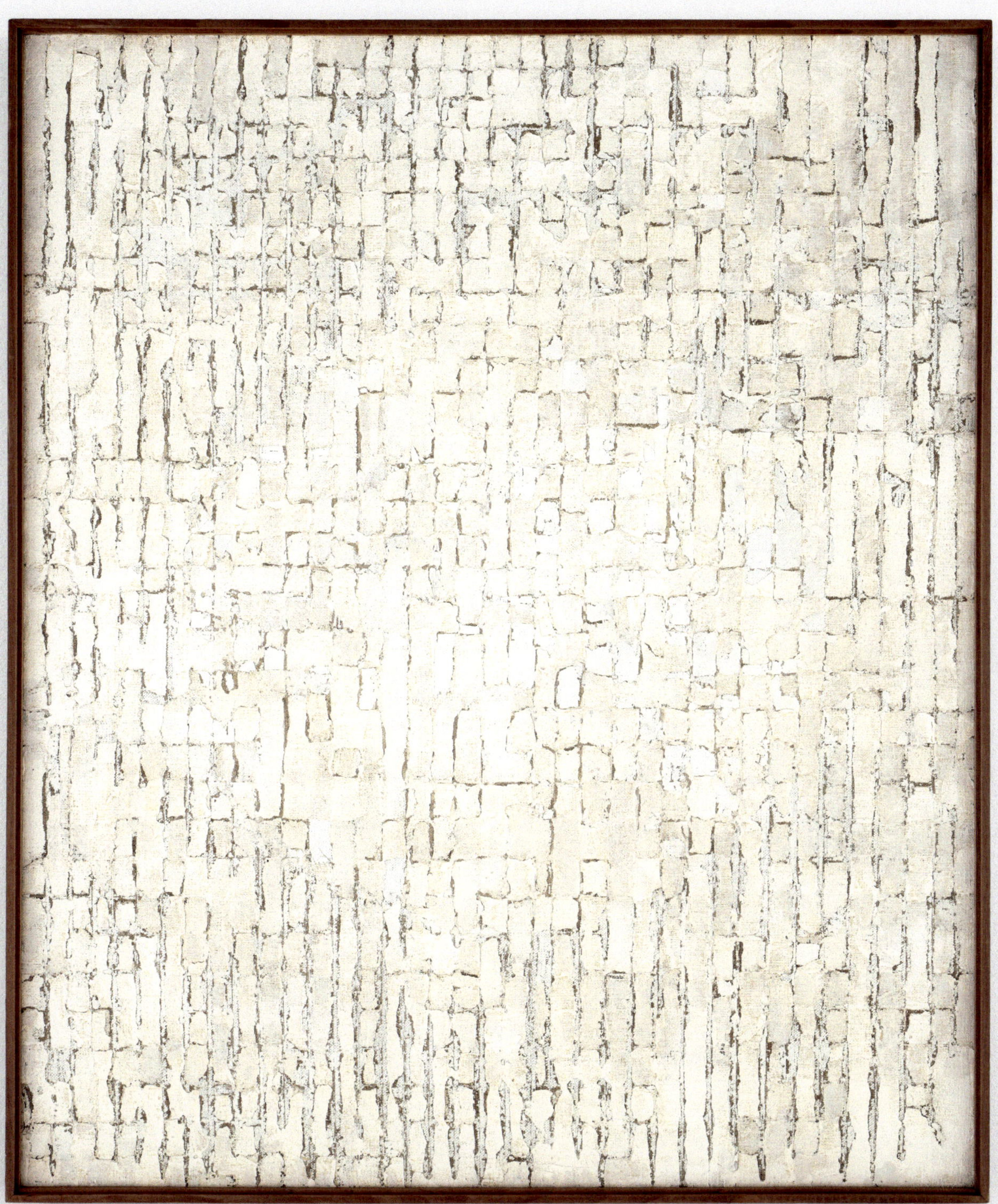

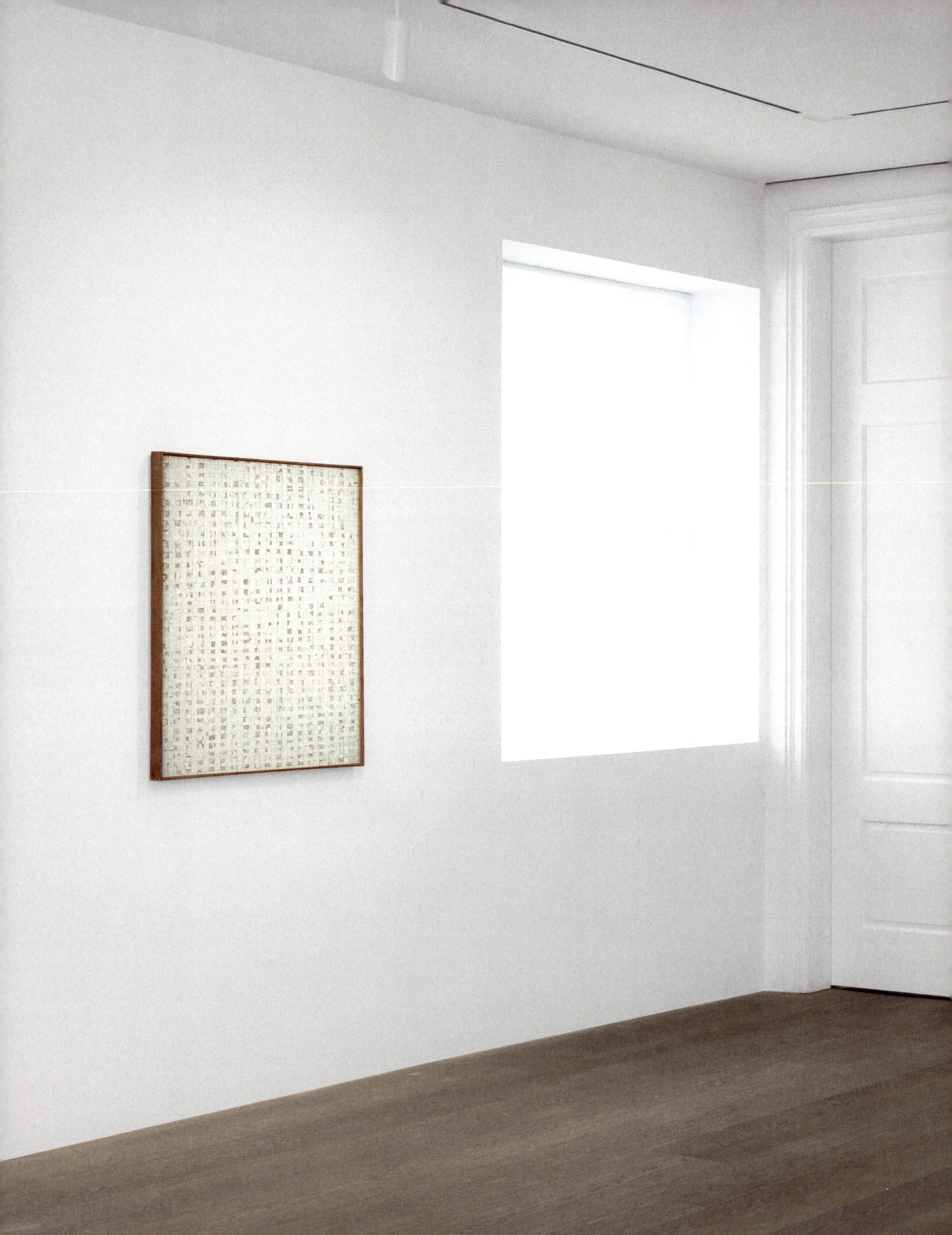

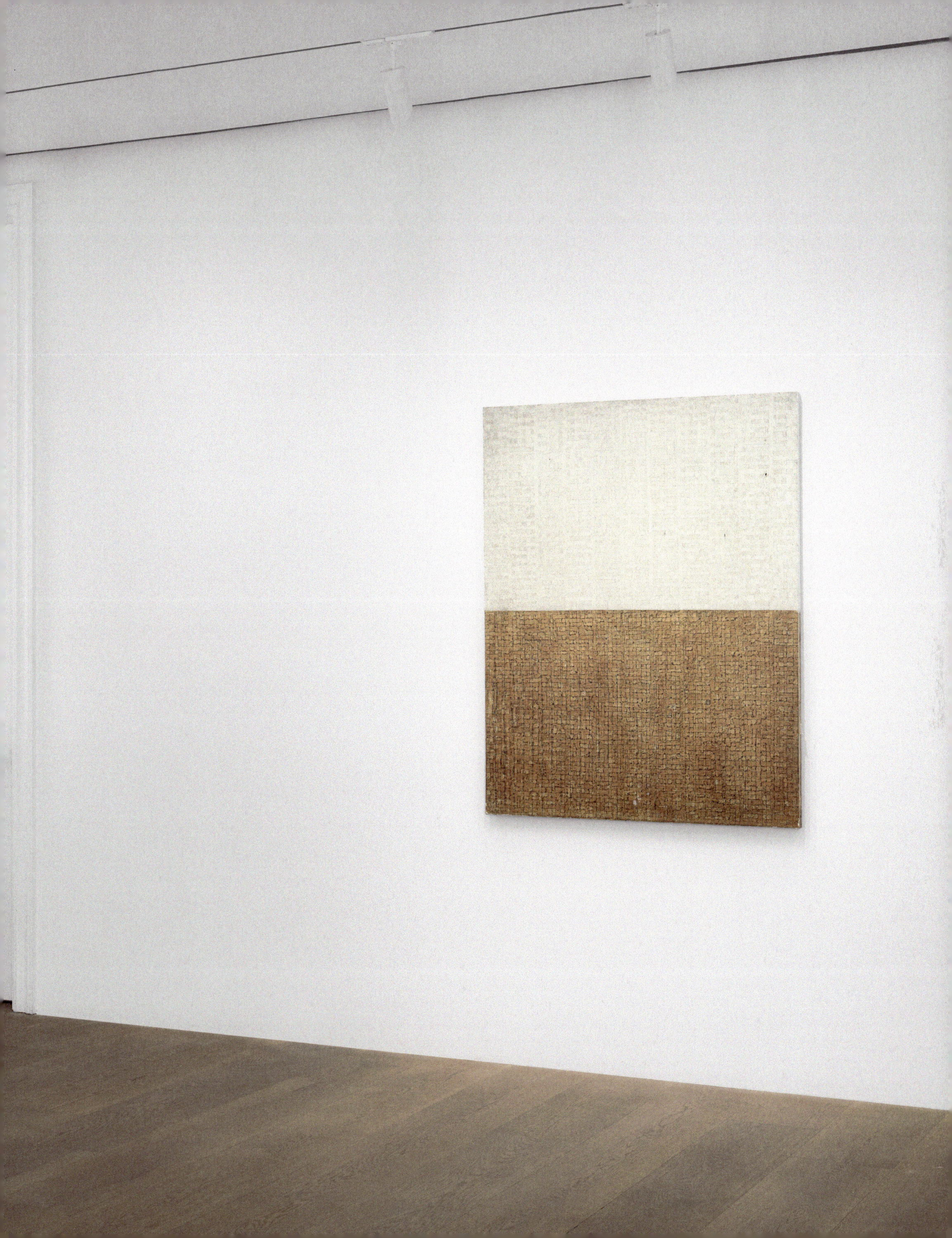

UNTITLED 77-8

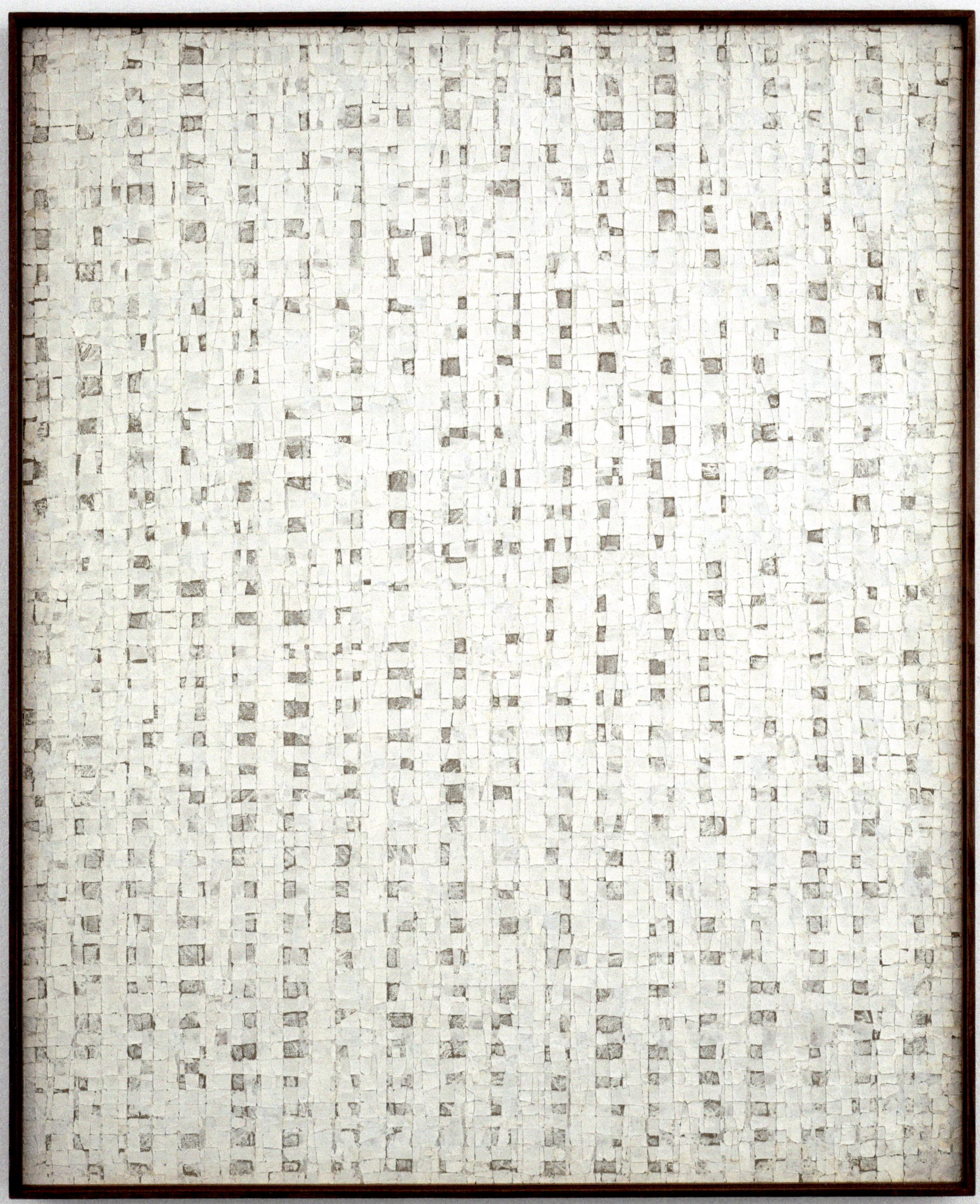

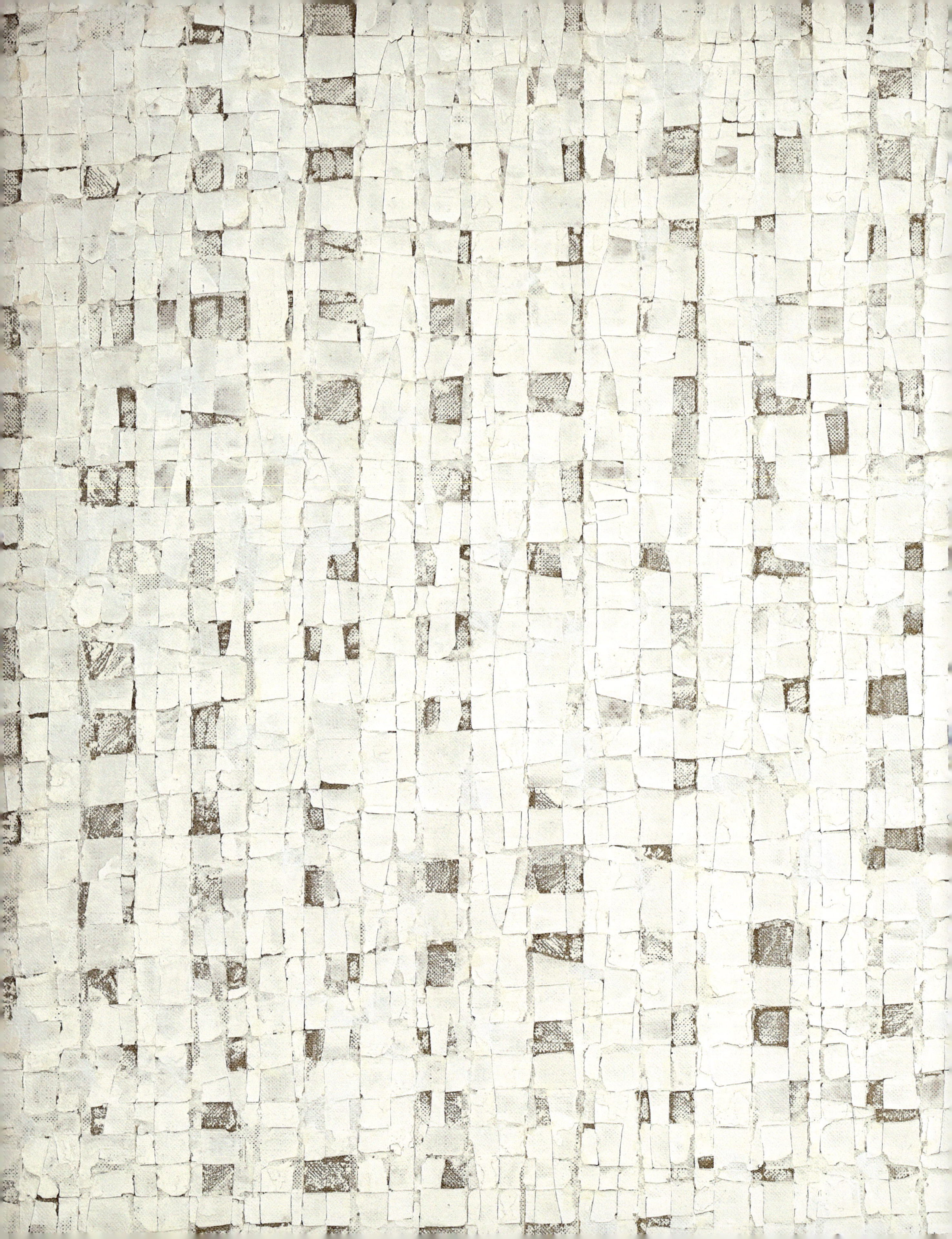

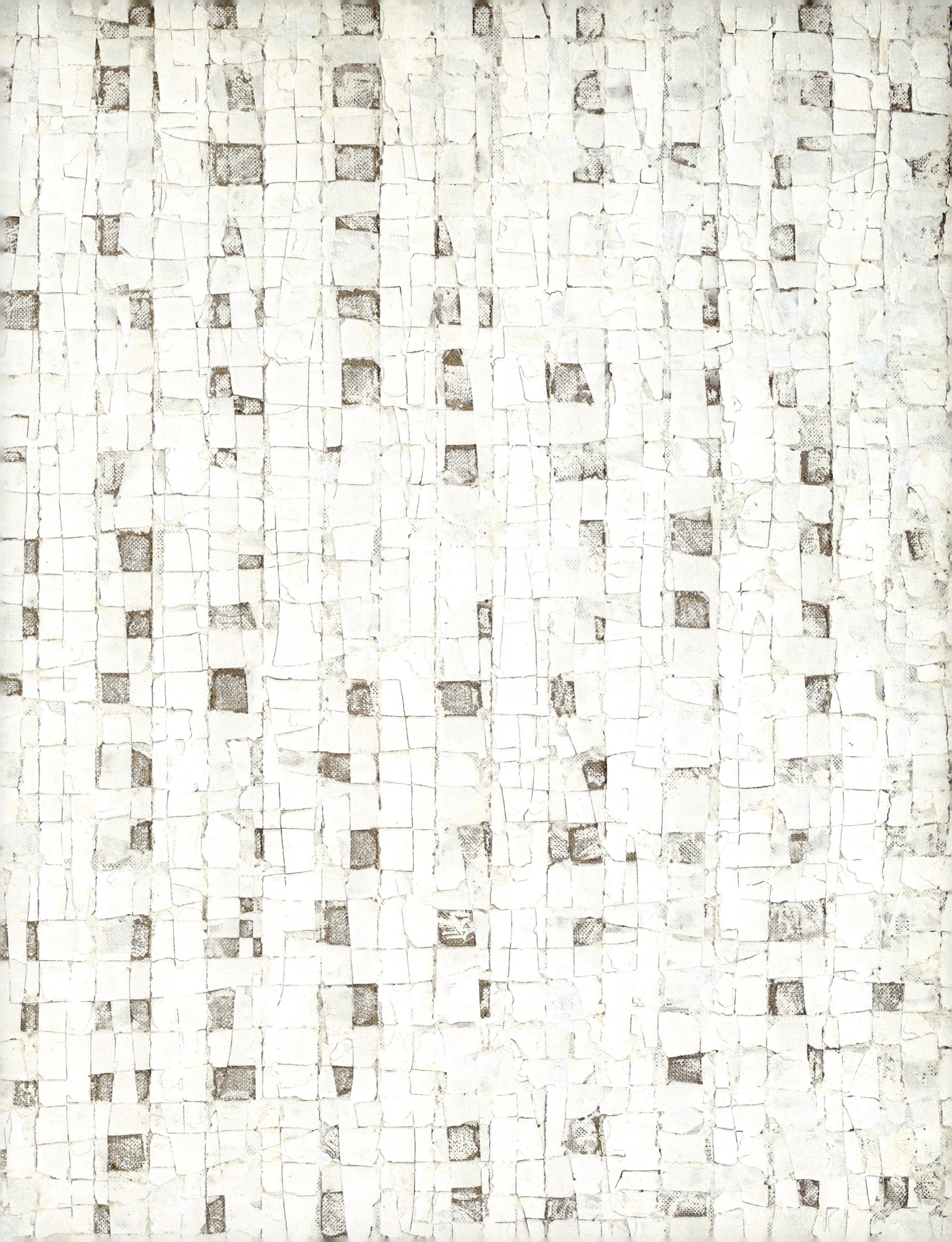

UNTITLED 78-11-29

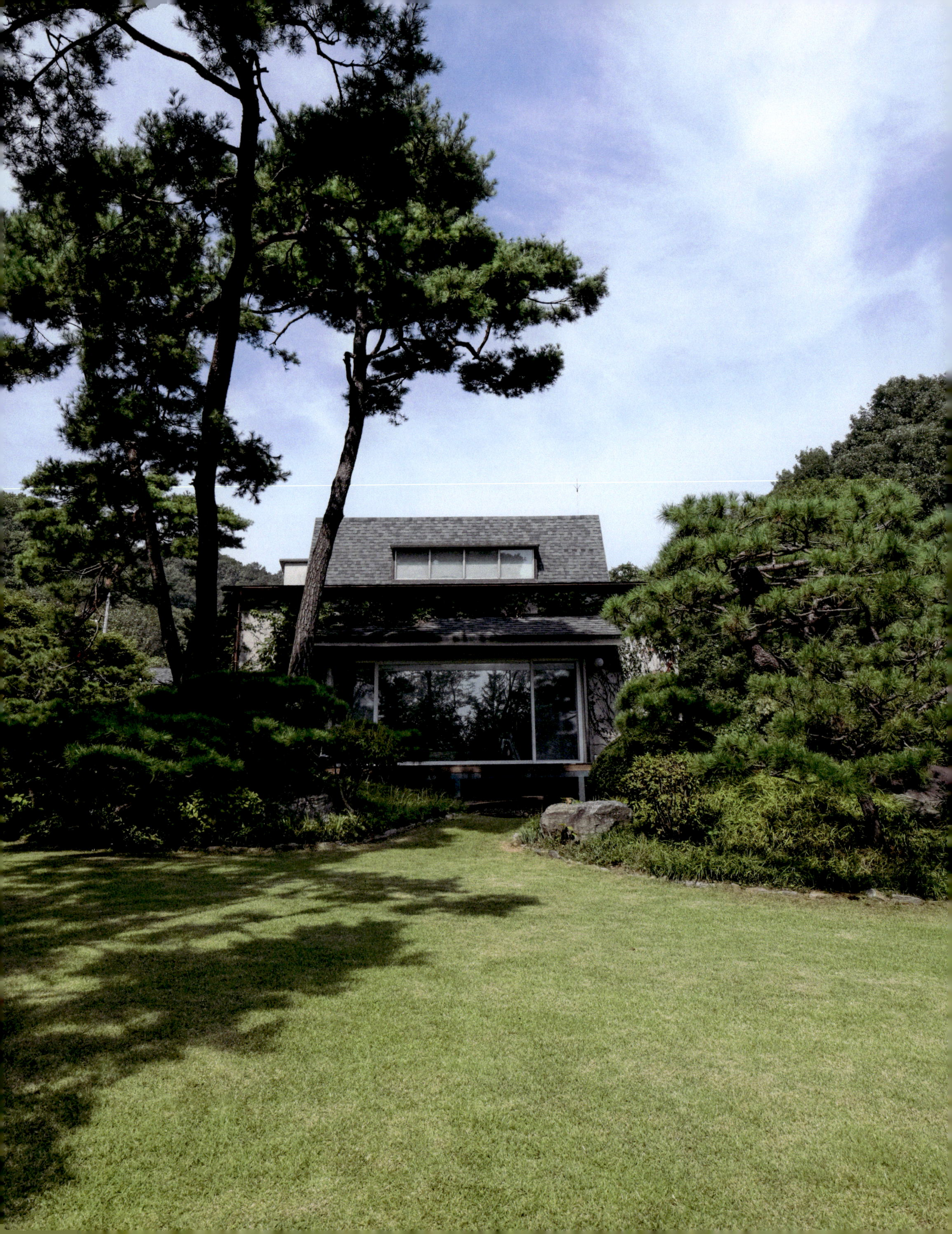

HOW YOU BECOME FREE:
A CONVERSATION WITH CHUNG SANG-HWA
BONA YOO

Bona Yoo Last time we were here, you emphasized how this work is especially meaningful for you (*Work 65-2*; page 21). So, I would like to start out by asking you to tell me more about it.

Chung Sang-Hwa I believe it's from the 1960s?

BY 1965, I believe.

CSH '65. Right. It was the Informel years. The Korean War had just ended. It was a period in which the younger generation experienced a lot of pain, troubled by the ensuing chaos. Therefore, the global trends at the time were strongly influenced by Art Informel. A group of us in the Korean art world who followed the movement first organized the Modern Art Association, called *hyundai mihyup*. Our movement, which comprised several members, is what we now know as Informel.

This work was made during that period. At the time, my focus was not on finding the right paint and putting it on the canvas, but rather the process of applying, eliminating, and reapplying paint on the surface, and ultimately, the construction of the surface through this repetition.

BY And this next work (*Work 69-A*; page 29) from 1969.

CSH Right before the 1970s. This work was about the composition of the picture, about circular forms, then examining the space, or a kind of a plane that emerges by eliminating the spatiality of those circular forms. Plane and space, you see? This work was created by repeatedly erasing and repainting the circular forms in my own way, and through the process, the space and plane of the painting came into form.

BY I find this work to be quite representative of your oeuvre. There are also the frottage works, of course, but your core process of removal and reapplication precedes them. You use both processes in this work from 1978 (*Untitled 78-11-29*, page 61).

CSH You can see the new changes here. I rolled up the whole canvas and folded it to create the cracks. I made the vertical and horizontal grid and repeated the process of eliminating and reapplying. Through repetition, a new plane emerged.

My work at this time was strictly focused on the construction of the flat surface. In this work, I applied *hanji* [traditional Korean paper] on the bottom half of the canvas and used graphite to create a frottage, as a way to visually define the flatness. I wanted to look at the contrast between the bottom and top half of the work. This was a very important point in my career.

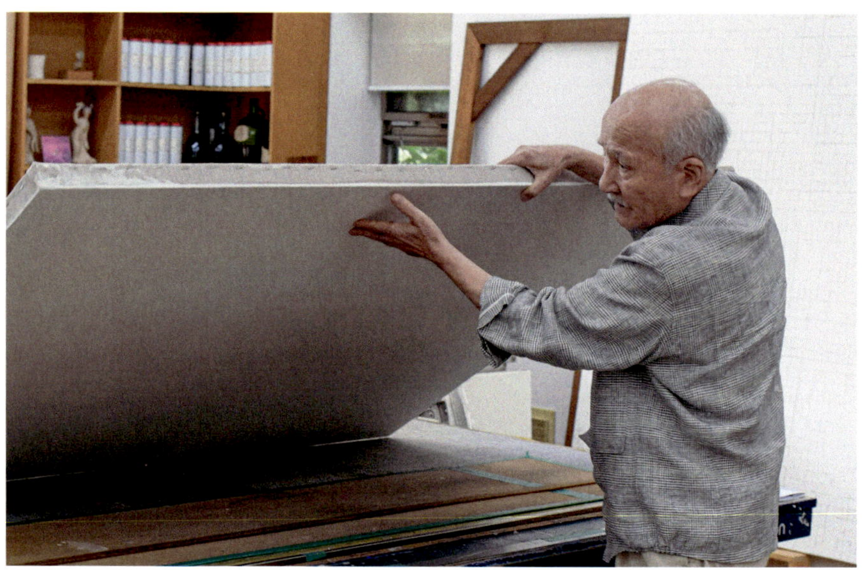

1. Chung applies the first layer of powdered kaolin to a canvas in his studio, Yeoju, South Korea, 2019

BY It does seem to mark a shift in your creative development, as the consideration of materiality, surface, and process converge. People are always curious about your process. Could you explain the steps you take, from start to finish?

CSH First of all, I prepare the canvas myself. I don't use pre-stretched canvases, I need my canvases to be free in order to paint. All of this has to be done in a comfortable, free setting. This is the secret to my process.

   The first step is applying the [animal] glue, then white [paint]. Both oil-based and water-based paint work fine. Next is applying the kaolin, which is in powder form (fig. 1). Then, there is this glue, or bond, that I use. This type of glue is used by carpenters for woodworking.

   I mix the kaolin and the glue in a 2:3 ratio and dissolve them in water. I apply this solution on the canvas with a brush. Not just one or two layers—I repeat the process about ten to twelve times, letting it dry and then reapplying, until the thickness of the painted surface reaches about .5 mm. When it reaches that thickness, it hardens. Once it hardens, I remove the canvas from the support. As you can see, once I remove the canvas I flip it over, make a grid on the other side, and

fold it (fig. 2). This folding process is like making the delicate pleats of a woman's skirt in traditional Korean clothing. I fold the canvas evenly to create the cracks, but they all come out differently (fig. 3). I allow chance to take over, even though I plan everything ahead. Through this process of eliminating and reapplying, the work comes into shape. I cannot explain every detail for the sake of time, but I am sure you can understand the overall process.

BY Are there particular principles driving this impulse? The repetition of eliminating and reapplying—what goes through your mind during this process?

CSH There is no need for explanation. The process is about the absolute elements that construct the flat surface. It is simply the instinct of the artist to carry this out. You are completely immersed in the process and you just let it happen. There is no need to overthink, but at the same time each and every step is thoughtfully executed. Sometimes I would fail in the process and have to start over. At times the work just collapses. But when that happens, you need to maintain the attitude that you can always rebuild.

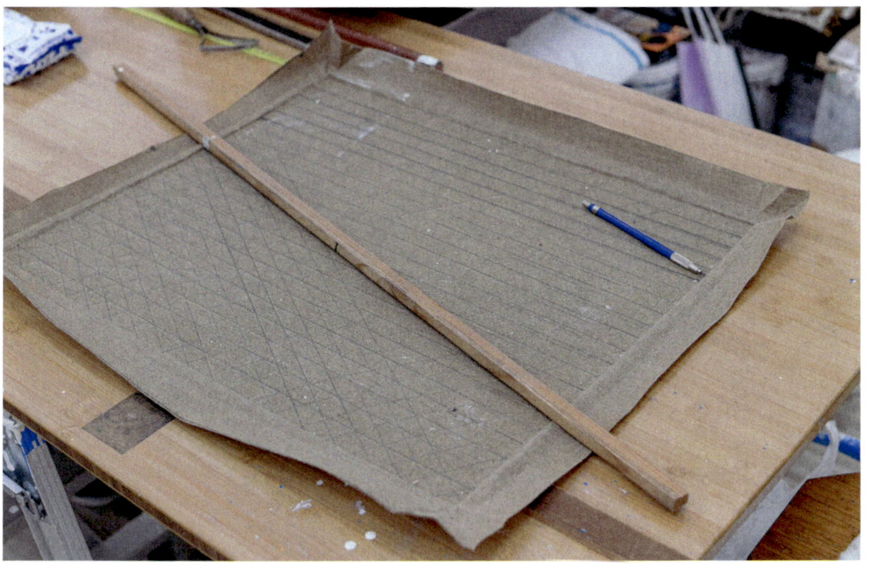

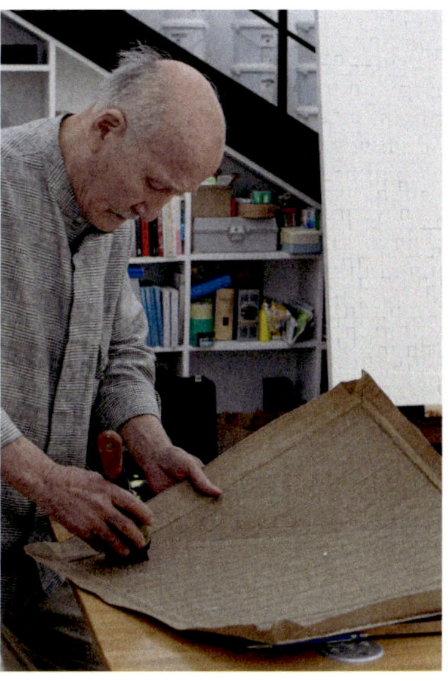

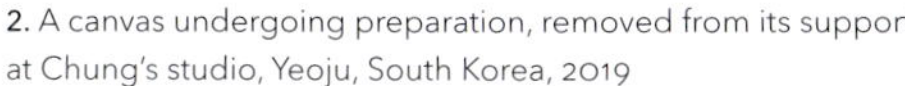

2. A canvas undergoing preparation, removed from its support at Chung's studio, Yeoju, South Korea, 2019

3. Chung folds a canvas in his studio, Yeoju, South Korea, 2019

In my work, the process of eliminating and applying are the same—completely equal to each other. As the work comes together, you can see the surface take shape—the highs and lows within the flat surface. In the end, it is all about the overall feeling that the canvas delivers, and the artist should always be mindful of that. At the same time, I need to think about details of the highs and the lows at all times.

BY In the past, you've described yourself as an "artisan." Has control of the entire production process always been important to you?

CSH Yes, from the very beginning. I began my career in the 1950s, and have since made everything myself, starting from the canvas. I always believed that an artist should be in total control of his materials. You can create an artwork with premade materials, but my personal opinion is that an artist should truly own his medium, subject, and everything about his work. That is how you create something that is completely your own.

Of course, when I was a student, I also used premade materials like paint, but I quickly moved on from this stage. An artist needs materials that are all

his own. That is how you become free. People say that my working process is very exhausting, but I always feel comfortable and free when I work. This is how I can work on these paintings, even though they are very time-consuming.

Sometimes a painting will keep me up all night and make me feel completely drained, yet I still have to do it. Of course, I cannot work that late anymore, because my health is not in great shape. Though they may not appeal to everyone, all of the works here were created with that same intensity.

BY You say that every artist needs to find his own medium. For you, I believe this is kaolin, which is usually associated with porcelain. How did you first become interested in this material?

CSH It was by coincidence. When I was a student at Seoul National University, we were always short on supplies. We could not afford to buy paint back then. When we would run out of paint, we used to buy this powder called *jitan* [a type of charcoal] and mix it with oil to make paintings. That was the beginning—buying powdered materials and mixing them with oil. However, there was

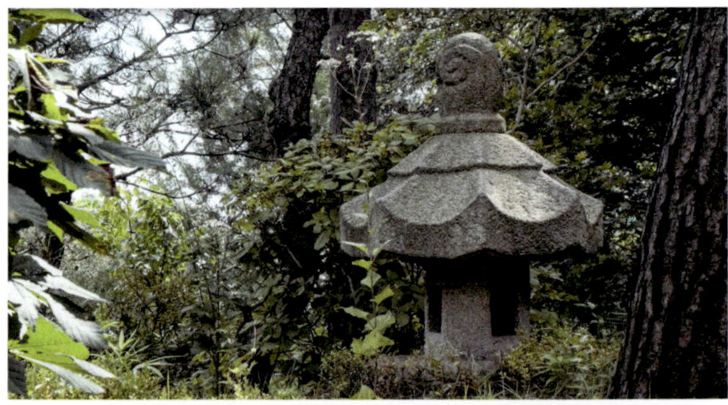
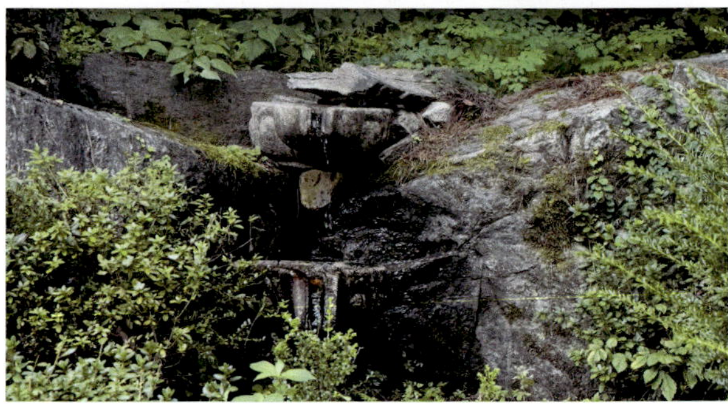

4a. and b. Landscape details in Chung's garden, Yeoju, South Korea, 2019

an upside to using these materials. For instance, kaolin is essentially powdered stone or clay, produced in the Gaoling region of China. The best part of this material is that it does not spoil or change over time.

When you are a young student, your mind is filled with curiosity. In the end, this is how I came across the material that remains the core of my practice to this day. How I work with kaolin is entirely self-developed and I never passed the method on to anyone else. No one can imitate it. No one can, even if they tried. You have to know the material, the process, and the method. This is strictly mine, and I take great pride in it.

BY The advantages of working alone are evident here, in this peaceful studio in Yeoju, where you work surrounded by nature (figs. 4a, b). What attracted you to this location?

CSH I was born and raised in the city. The city has everything of this world, and I have seen it all. I've been to France, the United States, Japan, and most countries in Europe. However, I wanted to find out who I am, what I am within this unspoiled nature. This thought is what brought me here. When I first came here, there was not a single house around.

I wanted to know about myself, my work, and what it all means in nature. I wanted to explore the relationship between nature, my work, and myself as an artist. That is why I came to this quiet place in the mountains. That was the only reason. Nothing else. It wasn't because I wanted to live comfortably. It was because I am an artist.

I wanted to create art surrounded by nature, understanding and appreciating the precious value of nature.

I didn't really have money when I first moved here, and the area was developed long after that. Even now, it makes me happy to think about what I have, which is being able to work as an artist in tune with nature at all times. I don't think any of my work can exist without nature.

BY I feel the influence of nature strongly in your art, and I'm sure most people do.

CSH I certainly hope so. Myself, my works, everything—we are all part of this universe.

BY I imagine that conviction has carried you through many decades of your practice. Going back to your earlier years, I would like to ask about the time you spent in Paris and Japan. How did those cultures and the people there affect your work (figs. 5, 6)?

CSH I am not sure. I can't say exactly how they affected me. Nevertheless, my experiences in Paris and Japan were a kind of awakening within myself—a subconscious awakening. Looking back, I ask myself: Why did I go there? What does it mean that I lived all those years in

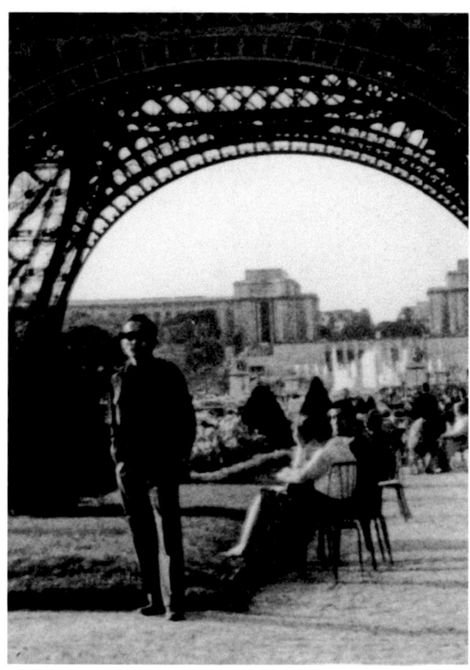

5. Chung at the Eiffel Tower, Paris, 1968

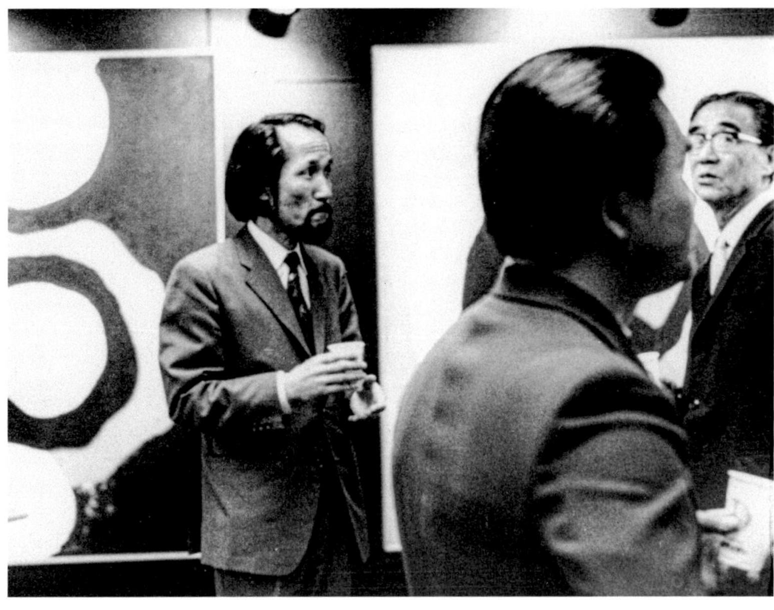

6. Chung at a solo exhibition of his work at Galerie Motomachi, Kobe, Japan, 1971

Paris? What was it like when I was in Japan? If I hadn't spent years in those places, at this age, my work would be—it's hard to say, but there is this feeling that comes and goes. It is a part of my living. There are certain inner conflicts when I work. My experiences of what Japan was like, France was like, and the US was like—those stay in my mind all the time. As an artist, to see the world is a good thing, an invaluable asset. However, when you see the bad, it only leads to bad things. Don't look at the bad. Only look at the good and follow in that path.

BY Is there anything in particular that you remember from your experiences in those countries?

CSH What I remember is only my work. I am an old man, and everything else has faded. My work is what remains with me now.

BY But you might say that those memories, though faded, remain in your work—especially the positive memories from your time abroad.

CSH Right.

BY Your garden is so beautiful. Was the stream always here?

CSH Yes, I didn't touch the landscape much. It is as it was when I first got here. I love it. I moved here for these [*gestures to trees and water*]. I planted these pine trees. They were not here before.

BY They look at home there. This must be a wonderful place to live and work.

CSH I brought all of these trees from elsewhere and planted them. It is so nice when you sit here during the summer. The landscape is amazing from here, and you can see the mountains far away. I take a walk out here all the time. I love the view from this angle. Beautiful, right? My favorite view. Look, there is absolutely nothing out there (page 73).

I just want to know who I am within all of this. Along with my works. There is not much to my everyday life here—nothing special.

BY A lot of energy went into planting a garden that looks so natural. Do you still work on it yourself?

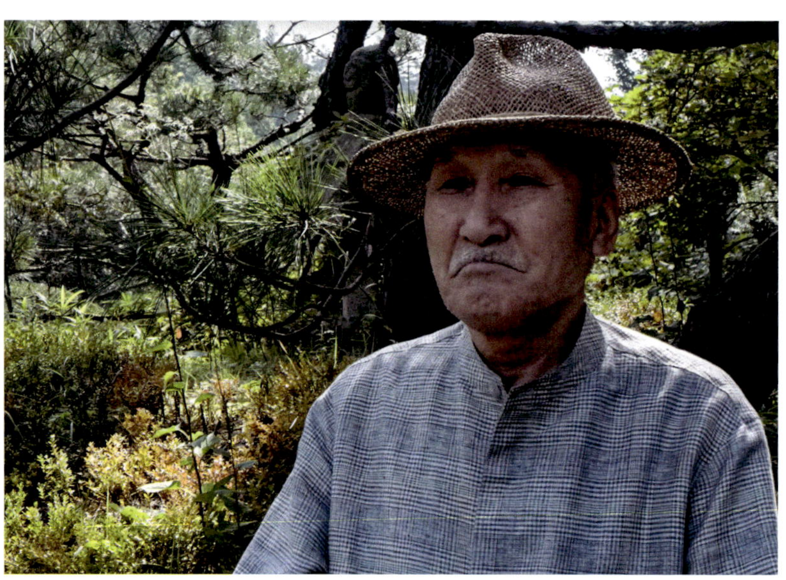

7. Chung in his garden, Yeoju, South Korea, 2019

8. Poster for the exhibition *Jeunes Peintres Coréens* [Young Korean Painters], on view at Galerie Lambert during the 3e Biennale de Paris, Paris, 1963

CSH I used to mow the lawn as exercise, but I can't anymore. Now I hire help, and my daughter helps out as well.

Come sit over here. This is the spot with the best view, where I sit with my guests (fig. 7). I talk about art with my artist friends, and sit around with my students. People love this garden. I came to live surrounded by this nature. As I said before, I wanted to question what I am and who I am. For me, to make paintings within this environment is an attempt to find that answer. As you know, Mr. Gorvy visited me here and probably thought that my thinking was different from others. I appreciate his interest.

BY I know he was very taken with the tranquility you have surrounded yourself with—as am I. When you first moved here, did you imagine that your garden would look like this?

CSH No. I looked after it for twenty-five years. The stones, the pond—I did everything myself. I poured my heart and soul into everything here. This small pond here is beautiful. There is a big goldfish in there. My students are astonished by this garden, and it makes me happy to see that they appreciate it.

Come sit here and rest. Look at those mountains. They look like a folding screen. When I feel tired while working in the studio, I come out here and take a walk.

BY When you were young, did you appreciate nature as you do now?

CSH I was too busy to think about anything, trying to make ends meet. It was after the Korean War, when I got into Art Informel. I cannot even describe the emotional pressures of that period. Now I live in peace, and Korea is a much more stable place. Everything is rebuilt. In those days, my body would ache and my mind would feel irritated for no reason, and so was my art. These days I feel calm, and so are my paintings.

BY So it's safe to say that throughout your life, your experiences have been directly reflected in your work.

CSH Right. I used to be very vocal about things when I was a teacher, but these days I rarely go out. I don't want to meet people. I want to stay here and paint until my last day. That is all I want. I don't even want to go to Seoul. Let's move on [*begins walking through garden*]. I planted all these pine trees. Look at this pond. Its shape is like the map of Korea. The water never dries up here. It is small but I am very fond of it. Try this [*holding a tree branch*]. It's gooseberry, from the trees in my garden. Take a bite.

BY Do you ever go over there when you are out on your walks [*gesturing to a distant area*]?

CSH Sure. I go everywhere. Let's go back inside. This is the poster from my exhibition in Paris [*points at poster on a wall in the studio*; fig. 8].

BY I would love to hear more about your early career. Was your education at Seoul National University a formative experience for you? Or did you establish your working process after your formal training ended?

CSH I would not be making the paintings I make today without my years in college. I am not saying that everyone needs to go through the college experience, but it certainly helped me. As you know, I am very strict on process, and I really tried my best during all four years of college. I was determined not to fall behind.

BY Those were very hard times.

CSH Right. It was difficult just to put food on the table, but I had to buy paint and keep painting.

BY You showed talent from a very young age. When did you start actually making art?

CSH I started drawing when I was in eighth grade. I had an interest early on, and I tried very hard all through my college years so that I wouldn't fall behind. You have to work hard. You are what you make of yourself and will get nowhere without effort. I'm trying to think of other people from my graduating class in college who are still working as artists, but no one comes to mind. There were about twenty-six of us. Seoul National University was difficult to get into, but the world after school was just as tough. Most of us, including myself, had to find day jobs to make ends meet.

I began teaching at a teachers' college right after graduating. The head of the college came to see the dean at my school and asked him to recommend a student. The dean recommended me, and that was how I was hired. It was a very special privilege, and because of this, I was able to continue painting through the tough times. Those were very difficult times in Korea.

BY What were your students like? What was your approach to teaching?

CSH It was a big responsibility, because you were teaching students who would become teachers to children in elementary schools. You had to be a positive influence. Later, I also taught at the Seoul Arts High School, and it was rewarding to see my students move on to college. Overall, I taught for about fifteen years. I began right out of college, because it was the only way I could afford to continue my painting. I had to spend most of my salary on art supplies, I couldn't provide much for my children. Those were challenging times [*laughs*].

BY In looking at your art from the early years to the present, one aspect that stands out is your interest in surface—which one could say is the most fundamental aspect of painting. What makes the surface so compelling for you?

CSH The surface, or rather the picture plane, has been a very important element since my student years. At first you are afraid to face the canvas in front of you, but as you train yourself, you learn to communicate with it—to communicate through your heartbeat. Once you can do that, it means you are confident.

The paintings I have been working on recently are all about flatness. My central focus is constructing flatness in the strictest sense. Flatness is a very important element at the core of modern painting. If you can't understand its value and conditions, then you are bound to run into trouble in your painting. You have to fully understand, accept, and acknowledge the concept in order to build your painting practice.

For me, the process of eliminating and reapplying is a way to explore and construct the flatness of the canvas. From there, I discover movement and also rhythm, like the rhythm or tempo of our breath. You can feel the painting breathe, as we ourselves do. You have to feel this. Of course, not everyone can understand or agree with me, but every artist has his own world. Viewers, in turn, should acknowledge that world when they look at an artist's work. You cannot look at every artwork the same way. You must understand the artist's world, as each artist has their own unique presence.

BY During your career, your journey has taken you across East and West. You spent time in Korea, Paris, Tokyo, and Kobe, then returned to Paris, and are now back in Korea.

CSH It's been over thirty years now. Of course, the environment and my work were different in each place. They were all different. When I look back, time spent in each place feels like a different period. With each block of time, a new change. These days, however, these time frames get muddled up in my mind, and feel like one big chunk of time.

There are two things I will miss most when I am no longer in this world: one is that I won't be able to paint, and the other is that I won't be able to experience this great nature. When I close my eyes, these are the only two things I will miss and regret—that I won't be able to see this nature, and that I won't be able to paint. Nothing else. This is why I try to fully immerse myself in painting while my eyes are open.

BY Is there anyone in particular who stands out in your memories from those years?

CSH There are a few [people], but they soon fade from memory. I am a stubborn man, and things just don't stay in my memory for that long. When I become frailer, perhaps I will think of someone. What is good is good, and you have to acknowledge that. I believe this to be true not just with people, but also with your work.

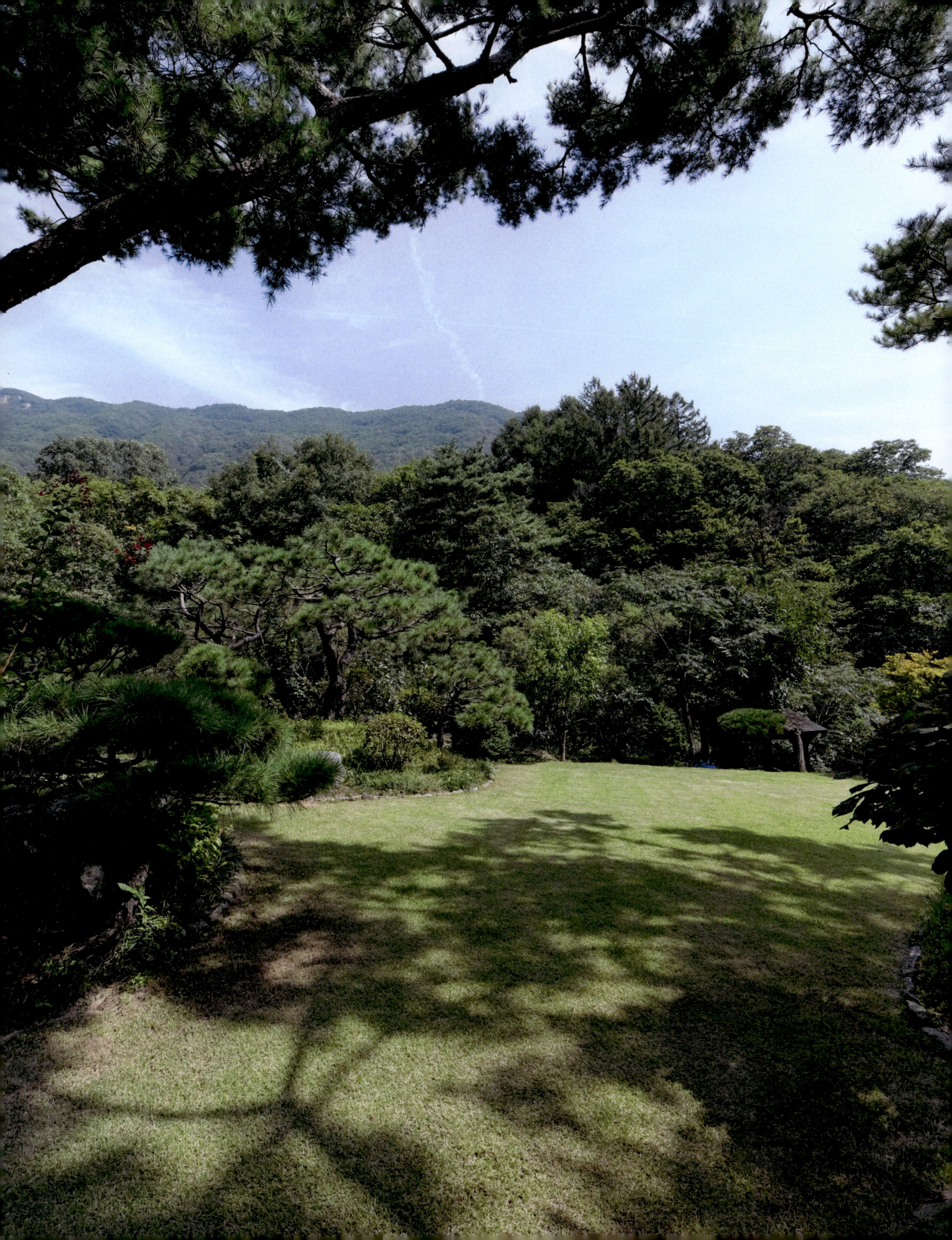

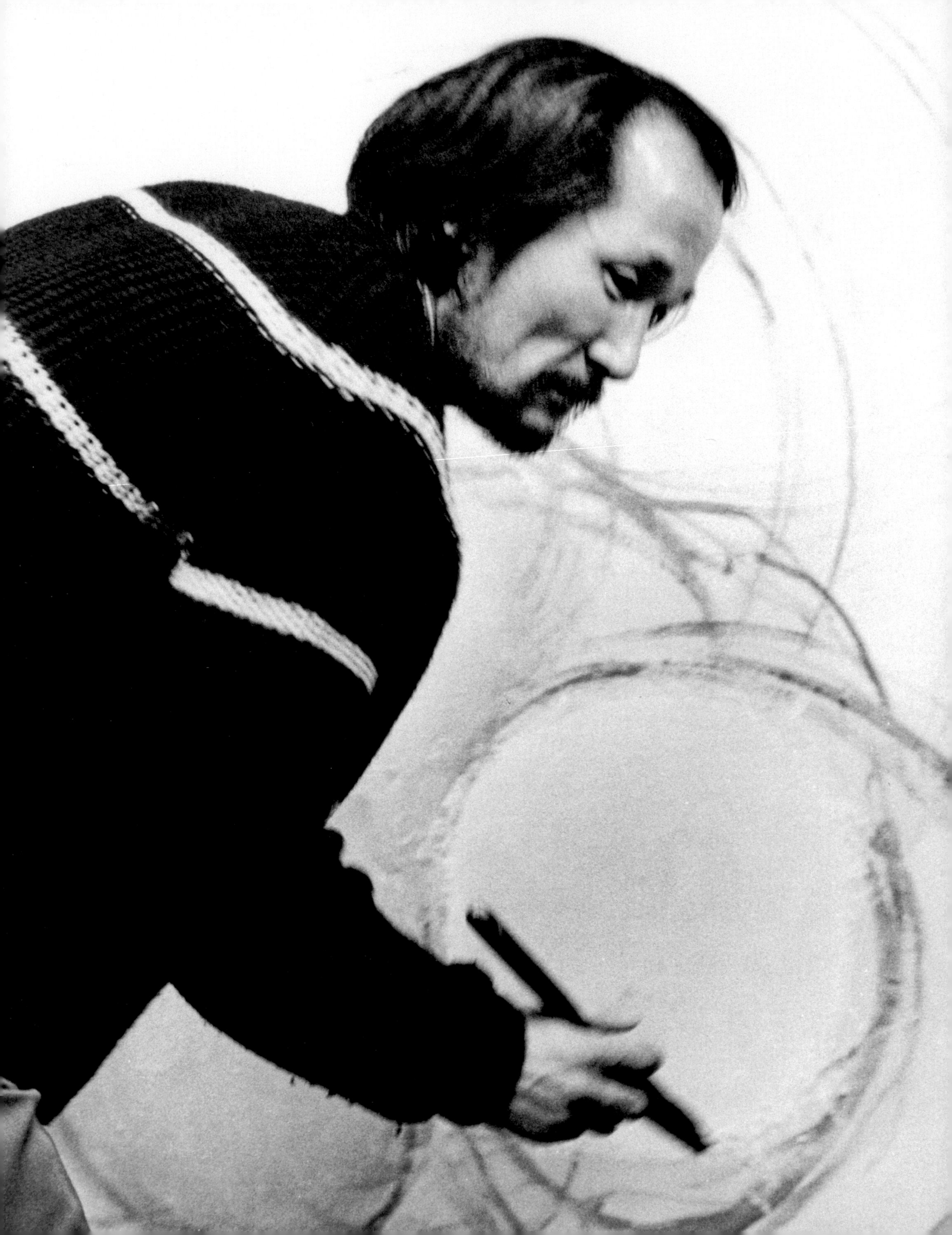

LIST OF WORKS

Pages 17; 18–19 (detail)

WORK 64-13 1964

Acrylic, kaolin, and oil on canvas
51 5/16 × 38 3/16 inches (130.3 × 97 cm)

Pages 21; 22–23 (detail); 14 (installation view)

WORK 65-2 1965

Acrylic, kaolin, and oil on canvas
63 7/8 × 51 5/16 inches (162.2 × 130.3 cm)

Pages 25; 26–27 (detail); 15, 37 (installation views)

WORK 68-32 1968

Acrylic and kaolin on canvas
46 × 28 5/8 inches (116.8 × 72.7 cm)

Pages 29; 30–31 (detail)

WORK 69-A 1969

Acrylic and oil on jute
57 1/4 × 44 1/8 inches (145.5 × 112.1 cm)

Pages 33; 34–35 (detail); 14 (installation view)

WORK 70-9-15 1970

Acrylic and oil on canvas
63 7/8 × 51 5/16 inches (162.2 × 130.3 cm)

Pages 39; 40–41 (detail); 15, 36 (installation views)

WORK K-3 1970

Acrylic, kaolin, and oil on canvas
64 × 51 5/16 inches (162.2 × 130.3 cm)

Pages 43; 44–45 (detail); 14 (installation view)

WORK O-A 1971

Acrylic and oil on jute
63 7/8 × 51 5/16 inches (162.2 × 130.3 cm)

Pages 47; 48–49 (detail)

WORK 72-B 1972

Acrylic and kaolin on canvas
25 5/8 × 20 7/8 inches (65.1 × 53 cm)

Pages 51; 52–53 (detail); 15 (installation view)

UNTITLED 75-10-8 1975

Acrylic on canvas
31 5/8 × 25 5/8 inches (80.3 × 65.1 cm)

Pages 57; 58–59 (detail); 54 (installation view)

UNTITLED 77-8 1977

Acrylic on canvas
35 13/16 × 28 5/8 inches (90.9 × 72.7 cm)

Pages 61; 62–63 (detail); 55 (installation view)

UNTITLED 78-11-29 1978

Acrylic, graphite, and *hanji*
(Korean mulberry paper) on canvas
51 5/16 × 38 3/16 inches (130.3 × 97 cm)

Published on the occasion of the exhibition

CHUNG SANG-HWA
EXCAVATIONS, 1964–78

ĹG
LÉVY GORVY

November 11, 2019–January 18, 2020
909 Madison Avenue
New York, NY 10021
+1 212 772 2004
levygorvy.com

February 28–April 25, 2020
22 Old Bond Street
London W1S 4PY
+44 203 696 5910
levygorvy.com

Founders: Dominique Lévy and Brett Gorvy
Senior Partner: Emilio Steinberger
Senior Director: Lock Kresler
Director: Bona Yoo
Director of Exhibitions: Clara Touboul
Associate Director of Exhibitions: Émilie Streiff
Publications Manager: Amelia Brown
Exhibitions Manager: Cristina Tafuri
Researchers: Hyunjee Nicole Kim and Courtney Fiske
Registrar: Maggie Merrell
Gallery Assistant: James Steele

In collaboration with Gallery Hyundai, Seoul, Korea

GALLERYHYUNDAI

President: Hyung-teh Do
Director: SungEun Kim
Creative Director: Jaeseok Kim

All works by Chung Sang-Hwa © 2020 Chung Sang-Hwa.
Courtesy Lévy Gorvy, New York, and Gallery Hyundai, Seoul
Publication © 2020 Lévy Gorvy, New York, and Gallery
Hyundai, Seoul

Design: McCall Associates, New York
Printing and Binding: Trifolio SRL, Verona
Editing: Susan Delson

ISBN: 978-1-944379-33-9

Printed and bound in Verona and available through
ARTBOOK | D.A.P.
75 Broad Street, Suite 630, New York, NY 10004
Tel: (212) 627-1999 Fax: (212) 627-9484

CAPTIONS

Cover: *Work O-A* (detail; 1971; page 43)
Page 6: Chung Sang-Hwa in his garden, Yeoju, South Korea, 2019
Pages 8, 12, 74: Chung in his studio, Kobe, Japan, 1970
Page 64: Chung's home, studio, and garden, Yeoju, South Korea, 2019
Page 73: Mountains seen from Chung's garden, Yeoju, South Korea, 2019

PHOTOGRAPHY CREDITS

Unless otherwise stated, the photographs and other images in this catalogue
are made available by the institutions or private lenders named as their owners
or by the artist. We have made every effort to locate all copyright holders. Any
errors or omissions will be corrected in subsequent editions.

ARCHIVAL PHOTOGRAPHY
Pages 6, 8, 12, 69 (left and right), 70 (right), 74: © Chung Sang-Hwa. Courtesy
Lévy Gorvy, New York, and Gallery Hyundai, Seoul

INTERVIEW PHOTOGRAPHY
Pages 64, 66, 67 (left and right), 68 (top and bottom), 70 (left), 73: Photographs
by Gary Yeh. Courtesy Lévy Gorvy, New York, and Gallery Hyundai, Seoul

EXHIBITION PHOTOGRAPHY
Cover and pages 14–15, 17, 18–19, 21, 22–23, 25, 26–27, 29, 30–31, 33, 34–35, 36–37, 39,
40–41, 43, 44–45, 47, 48–49, 51, 52–53, 54–55, 57, 58–59, 61, 62–63: Photographs by
Elisabeth Bernstein. Courtesy Lévy Gorvy, New York, and Gallery Hyundai, Seoul

TEXT CREDITS

"Chung Sang-Hwa: Positive Passivity" © 2020 Barry Schwabsky

Excerpt entitled "Like the Very First Time" by Shin Young-Bok / English translation
© 2020 David McCann

"How You Become Free: A Conversation with Chung Sang-Hwa" © 2020 Bona Yoo
with the collaboration of Jaeseok Kim / English translation © 2020 Nayoung Cho

Our sincere gratitude to the team at the gallery, and our collaborators:
Clara Touboul and Émilie Streiff, whose expertise in orchestrating exhibitions
across time zones and languages has been invaluable; Amelia Brown, for her
efforts in compiling an elegant book; Hyunjee Nicole Kim and Courtney Fiske,
for their research; Cristina Tafuri, for her dedicated work in coordinating this
exhibition; and James Steele, for his assistance. To Mark Nelson and Elin Miller
of McCall Associates, Susan Delson, and Massimo Tonolli, thank you for your
steadfast commitment to our publications.